HOW
TO AFFORD
TIME OFF
WITH YOUR BABY

HOW TO AFFORD TIME OFF WITH YOUR BABY

101 Ways to Ease the Financial Strain

Becky Goddard-Hill

Vermilion
LONDON

3 5 7 9 10 8 6 4 2

Published in 2009 by Vermilion, an imprint of Ebury Publishing
A Random House Group Company

The Random House Group Limited Reg. No. 954009

Addresses for companies within the Random House Group can be
found at www.randomhouse.co.uk

A CIP catalogue record for this book is available from
the British Library

The Random House Group Limited supports The Forest Stewardship
Council (FSC®), the leading international forest certification organisation.
Our books carrying the FSC label are printed on FSC® certified paper.
FSC is the only forest certification scheme endorsed by the leading
environmental organisations, including Greenpeace. Our
paper procurement policy can be found at
www.randomhouse.co.uk/environment

Printed and bound in Great Britain by Clays Ltd, St Ives PLC

ISBN 9780091924294

To buy books by your favourite authors and register for offers visit
www.randomhouse.co.uk

For Frankie and Annalise – I wouldn't have missed a minute. You are my darling angels and I am so blessed to have you. Always know how special, smart, and wonderful you are. Mummy loves you.

Contents

Chapter 3: Have a Lovely Pregnancy

Chapter 4: Baby's Arrival

Chapter 5: Your Newborn Baby (0–6 months)

Chapter 6: Time to Think About You (0–6 months post-baby)

Chapter 7: Weaning, Walking and Wearing You Out (6–24 months)

Chapter 8: Staying Sane Through Those Terrible Twos

Chapter 9: Taking Care of Yourself (6–36 months post-baby)

Chapter 10: The Pre-School Years (3–5)

Chapter 11: Earning Money While Staying Off Work

If I had my child to raise all over again...
I'd finger paint more and point the finger less.
I'd do less correcting and more connecting.
I'd take my eyes off my watch and watch with my
    eyes.
I would care to know less and know to care more.
I'd take more hikes and fly more kites.
I'd stop playing serious and seriously play.
I'd run through more fields and gaze at more stars.
I'd do more hugging and less tugging.
I would be firm less often and affirm more often.
I'd build self-esteem first, and the house later.
I'd teach less about the love of power, and more
    about the power of love.

If I Had My Child to Raise Over Again by Diana Loomans is taken
from *100 Ways to Build Self-Esteem & Teach Values*. Reproduced
with kind permission. Diana Loomans © 2009.
For more information, visit www.dianaloomans.com

Introduction

Do you associate having a baby with huge outgoings? Do you wonder how you will afford all that baby paraphernalia (pram, cot, toys, endless supplies of nappies, car seats, activities and babysitting costs), as well as having time off work on less or no money at all? In 2008, the cost of bringing up a child from birth to the age of 21 was put at £186,032.[1] With that kind of figure, it's a miracle that anyone can afford to have children at all! What's more, such costs can deter couples from starting a family until they feel more financially secure. But – and here's the good news – babies don't have to be expensive, and this book will show you how you can afford time off with your baby.

Whether you are planning to get pregnant, are already pregnant or are a new mum on a reduced income, you will find a host of inspirational but easy-to-achieve ideas within this book to help you cope with everyday life while your children are small and your earning power is reduced. From managing expenditure and maximising savings, to finding bargains and even earning some extra cash – all the tips are do-able while caring for your baby on a full-time basis. Just as importantly, there's plenty of great advice on how to have fun with your baby on a budget.

I am not proposing you resort to making a baby bed in the bottom drawer (though that's always good as a last resort!) or inserting newspaper inside your babies' clothes to keep them warm. What I am proposing are creative solutions for modern times – solutions designed to make your life easier. I have arranged the book so that you can dip in for inspiration, as and when you need it.

This book spans the time from pregnancy through to preschool. It includes, among many other things, how to have a creative Christmas on a budget, alongside how to dress your child beautifully without breaking the bank. It provides thrifty ways to meet both your baby's needs and your needs; you can reduce your expenditure without reducing your quality of life. At the back of the book (see page 239) is an extensive Resource Bank, with details of where to buy, sell, save and get support – I hope having all these websites, phone numbers and useful books at your fingertips will save you precious time and energy, when caring for your baby is probably leaving you with few of your own resources.

This book is the culmination of how I learned to live happily on significantly less money during the five years I spent off work with my babies. It is a compilation of advice from me, other mums, research and the results of trial and error. My story is interwoven throughout and I hope you will be inspired to try the things that worked for me – and manage to avoid those that did not.

HOW DID I GET HERE? THE LAST FIVE YEARS

I was a social worker by profession and I worked in a Social Services training department teaching childcare issues (such as child protection, bullying, child development and communicating with children) to social care workers. I had been in my job about four years and enjoyed it: it was interesting and varied, and I had some great colleagues. Equally, I was thrilled to become pregnant and just so excited about meeting my new baby.

However, I was the major earner at that time; my husband is, and was, self-employed as an IT consultant (it sounds lucrative but it's a pretty new business and still developing). Our joint annual income was about £42,000. We lived in a suburb and had a standard (by which I mean expensive) mortgage, so there was never any question about my not going back to work. I needed to, as far as we could see, to keep our quality of life and that was that. The plan was that I would go back four days a week after my maternity leave. After visiting countless nurseries (and quizzing each at great length; it's my social work training – I drove them mad!) we finally selected one and paid a hefty deposit. But what our plan failed to foresee was how I would feel about my baby and that he would have specific care needs during his first year.

Frankie was a tiny dot when he was born and needed time in a special care unit. We were advised to keep him out of nursery for his first year as he was small and so vulnerable to illness. That was fine – my work agreed that I could have a year off and we immediately took a six-month mortgage break. We knew it would be tough, but we could cut back and we thought we could just about manage. Secretly, I was very pleased that my six-month maternity leave was to become a whole year off work.

What can I say? That first year was simply magical. By the time my son was six months old I was already agonising about returning to work. I talked to everyone I knew about what to do and I got a myriad of different opinions, ranging from 'It will wreck your career,' 'You'll never afford it' and 'You'll miss your luxuries' to 'It's the best thing you could ever do' and 'You'll never regret it', along with a variety of useful suggestions as to how we could afford to do this. As time moved on I was resolute about not going back to work: I was prepared to move house, downsize, sell my car, get a loan...anything, in fact, to enable me to stay home with my little one.

My husband, Jonny, who is definitely a risk-taker, believes firmly in following your heart. (He once bought a treasure map and dug for gold for six months in the Phillipine jungle – so he was *not* going to be a voice of reason.) He urged me to do what felt right. Thank goodness. Our joint annual income was about to dwindle to £15,000 and that was scary. How on earth were we going to afford this time off? We talked for hours about what we wanted and what was right for us. Luckily we thought and felt the same way. So, we made a plan. We would have to:

- talk to work about my options (perhaps I could do ad-hoc freelance work in the evenings or at weekends)

- look carefully at our finances
- be creative about each and every purchase
- access any benefits we could
- get our families and friends on board
- reduce our outgoings.

It all sounded a bit dreary. So, we factored into our plan that it was *not* going to be dreary; it was going to be full of fun and as far as possible we would not compromise our lifestyle, we would just do things differently.

I called work and, after some discussion, they agreed to me having a six-year career break but with the option to go back earlier. I felt incredibly fortunate. I know this is unusual, but then again there have to be some benefits to being in Social Work! I cancelled the nursery place I had booked (I lost my deposit, never pay a £200 deposit), we took a deep breath and four years later we are poor but happy and have had a ball. What's more, our family has grown with the arrival of Annalise; and we still find parenthood as marvellous as the first-time round (and a lot less expensive).

As I write, my son Frankie is five and my daughter is two. He has started school and her toddler years are in full swing. I have loved spending time with my children, during which I have run a small business teaching baby signing, stood at car-boot stalls, learned the wonders of eBay, book parties and skill sharing, and much, much more. To be honest, there have been tough times, but never too tough. I think we have become less materialistic and, as a result, much more creative and relaxed than we used to be. Our family has become a part of our community and we definitely have deeper, more productive friendships. It has been a journey of real discovery.

I hope your story and your journey will be just as exciting.

Becky Goddard-Hill

P.S. It's an important job

A friend once asked me if I didn't feel demeaned by the fact I was not a career woman. I told her I believed I was doing one of the best jobs in the world. What I should have said, much more poetically, was this...

> *A hundred years from now it will not matter what my bank account was, the sort of house I lived in or the kind of car I drove...but the world may be different because I was important in the life of a child.* [2]

However much time you are able to take off work with your baby, whether it is is six months or six years, I hope this book will contribute to making that precious time enjoyable, as well as affordable.

Footnotes

1. *Scholastic Education Plus*, 7 Jan 2008. www://magazines.scholastic.co.uk/content/1547
2. Forest Witcraft, 'Within My Power', *Scouting*, 1950. page 2.

CHAPTER 1

Pre-Birth: The BIG Considerations

I guarantee you it is easier than you think to afford to spend more time at home with your baby. All it takes is planning, action, creativity, organisation and, sometimes, a little bit of *chutzpah*. The best place to start is with your finances. Don't fret if things initially look a bit scary. In this chapter you will find simple, achievable ideas to cut down on the big bills and simplify your spending.

1. TAKE A LONG HARD LOOK AT YOUR FINANCES

Take stock of your financial situation; it's tempting to put this off, but don't. Instead, grab a big notepad and start jotting down some cold, hard facts. Use the table overleaf as a guide, but get out some recent bank statements to make it as accurate as possible.

Once the numbers are on the page, you should be able to fully examine your situation. Now you can see exactly what money is coming in and going out each month, you can take steps to reduce those non-essential payments.

Income		Outgoings	
What do you earn?		*Essential payments:*	Mortgage or rent
Any benefits? (See 3. Benefits: what could you be entitled to? page 28)			Council tax
What does your partner earn? (Will it cover all expenses if you're not earning?)			Water rates
			Gas
			Electricity
			Phone (and broadband)
			Food
			Travel
			Petrol
			Insurance (buildings, contents, car)
			Hair cuts
			Credit card payments
			Fund for car and house repairs
		TOTAL	
		Non-essential payments:	Subscriptions (to gym, TV service, museum membership, magazines etc.)
			Charity donations
			Retail therapy
			Beauty treatments (regular manicures, massages etc.)
			Holidays
		TOTAL	

Can you manage financially not to work, if that's what you want? Would a part-time arrangement be better? Explore all your options; maybe you just want six months or a year off, maybe two years, maybe more. What can you realistically afford to do?

I believe you will miss things much less than you think when you start to streamline your outgoings. We have made some easy and some not so easy changes. But they have never been as hard as I thought. For instance, I now get my hair coloured every 10 weeks rather than every six weeks – no one can tell and I save nearly £150 a year. 'Sky Sports is not an essential!' I've often cried to my husband, but that said three years on we do still have it. He reasoned he would spend more on beer if he had to go and watch the match at the pub. Hmmm.

In 2005 the average cost of bringing up a baby from birth to the age of five was put at £52,605. *Pregnancy & Birth* magazine, which commissioned the research, based it on the spending of the average parent in Mothercare, so if you factor in designer brands the costs just go up, up and up. This total equates to all the baby basics if bought new, plus the biggest expense of all – childcare. Childcare costs come in at about £30,000 or more over four years for a full-time nursery place. So, if you don't return to work, you can reduce this estimate by £22,605 just by looking after your own kids. Add to that, buying some cheaper or second-hand goods, borrowing items from friends or family or asking for them as gifts, and you could easily halve the remaining amount to about £10,000 over five years – now that is far more manageable.

Although you get paid for working (which is of course very handy), a job comes with its own associated costs, the primary one being childcare. Other, not insignificant, expenses may include:

- work clothes (bags, shoes etc.)
- travel
- lunches and coffees
- work functions
- collections for people leaving or having a baby
- personal grooming
- pre-packed meals or takeaways when you are too tired to cook
- cleaner.

If you are home with one baby you should have time to cook and clean yourself (although don't bank on this when your baby becomes a toddler or when baby number two comes along), thereby seriously minimising all the other costs.

So, in summary, work out what you can do without and what you definitely need to budget for. Once you know exactly how much income your life requires, you can calculate what you can afford to do about returning to work. Be courageous and expect to have to make some sacrifices and changes. Your baby will most definitely be worth it.

2. PUT YOUR FINANCES IN ORDER

It really helps if you can be financially sorted before you embark on the 'baby business'. You will not have much time to sort these things out once your little angel has arrived, so try and do as much as you can in advance – for the sake of both your purse and your stress levels. Below are some tips to get you started.

DO NOT PANIC ABOUT MONEY – Babies do not need much; babies have been around forever, throughout history and all over the world, in far less luxurious lifestyles than ours. What your baby needs really is very little.

PLAN FOR THE SHORT TERM – Remember financial decisions made now are just for the next few years. Your baby will be at school before you know it – by the age of four or five – and you can reassess your finances once you're back in the realms of paid employment.

GET PROFESSIONAL ADVICE – It may pay to visit an independent financial advisor or even one based at your bank to assess your situation and make suggestions for improvements. For example, I was paying a monthly charge for an account that gave me free travel insurance but I wasn't going away enough for it to be worthwhile. It took me several years to realise this before I switched to a free current account. Another bank charged us £35 every time we went overdrawn (even by £10) and would not let us have an authorised overdraft. We've since moved our joint account; so, occasionally being overdrawn no longer results in a very overpriced letter telling us about it. Check your bank is working for and not against you.

LOSE THE NON-ESSENTIALS – As we said earlier, it is also a good idea to cut out as many regular non-essential payments, such as standing orders, as you can – magazine subscriptions, charities (it's only for a while), the chocolate eaters' club (it exists!) gym memberships, etc. There are alternative ways to have fun, get fit and give to others, which we will look at later.

CURB YOUR SPENDING – Reduce your use of store cards (they are incredibly expensive if you can't pay off your whole balance) and try to reduce any other credit or store card debts significantly. Familiarise yourself with your payment dates; missing them can be more money down the drain in late payment charges. I was just two days late on a small credit card bill recently and was charged; my disorganised life had cost me £15. It's never happened again – I have so many better uses for £15.

STICK WITH THE ESSENTIALS – Whatever you do, don't cancel your life insurance, buildings and contents insurance or car insurance. If you ever need them and didn't have them it would be a financial disaster. Enough said.

CONSOLIDATE YOUR DEBTS? – To make it easier to budget from the start, you may prefer to put all your debt in one place and fix small monthly payments. Check out the deals being offered by reputable banks and building societies, but do be careful to read any small print. Also see www.moneysupermarket.com as they compare hundreds of loans and are continuously updated.

FREE UP YOUR SAVINGS – If you have savings tied up, look into moving them into a more accessible account. And it may be worth cashing in any premium bonds or other savings plans to reduce your debt.

GO WITH THE CHEAPEST – Don't just stick with what you know. Switch your insurance, phone and utilities to the lowest-priced providers. Do your research on this now and make that move. Check out some price-comparison websites (such as www.confused.com or www.uswitch.com), which offer a free service, and you could save literally hundreds of pounds. Take a look at the Review Centre (www.reviewcentre.com), which provides unbiased reviews of the various comparison services on offer.

WRITE EVERYTHING DOWN –You have probably heard it a thousand times but if you write down everything you spend for a whole week (and I mean everything) then you may find that a lot of your money is frittered away. For example, two coffees at a café, a magazine, four newspapers, a taxi instead of the bus, that pretty pink new nail varnish, a Danish pastry, a takeaway one evening and a bottle of wine, an emergency wash and blow-dry and that new scarf – all your little luxuries during a normal week could easily add up to about £80 (that's over £4,000 a year). Not one of the above purchases would strictly be necessary, yet all could slip into your week without seeming at all extravagant. Grab that big pad again, once it's there in black and white you can figure out where your money is going and so change some spending habits. (There are, however, in my opinion, always enough pennies for an emergency Kit Kat.)

See the Resource Bank (page 239) for more places to get inspiration for putting your financial house in order.

3. BENEFITS: WHAT COULD YOU BE ENTITLED TO?

Don't imagine you have to be on a low wage to get benefits; even the Queen is entitled to Child Benefit. Most couples earning less than £50,000 jointly are entitled to something. At particular times during my extended leave from work, I got almost as much in benefit payments as I would have earned working part-time (after childcare costs) all for staying home with my babies. Fantastic. Claim what you are due – there's no shame in accepting benefits, especially when you have probably paid a lot into the system and will do again. It is your turn right now to get something back. After all, you are doing the most important job in the world.

All female employees are entitled to a minimum of 26 weeks Ordinary Maternity Leave irrespective of how long they have worked for their employer. They are also entitled to a period of Additional Maternity Leave, which lasts for another 26 weeks. The maternity leave period is now 52 weeks in total if you want it to be.

Be sure to work out what you are entitled to as part of your planning process, you don't need to wait until your baby arrives. Knowing what you will be due can help you make those big decisions about how much time you will take off.

All the information listed in this section is correct as of April 2009; check the websites in the Resource Bank (page 246) for any updates.

Check the following benefits to see which you may be entitled to.

O Statutory Maternity Pay
O Contractual Maternity Pay
O Maternity Allowance
O Child Tax Credit
O Working Tax Credit
O Child Benefit
O Child Tax Fund Vouchers
O Matex

Statutory Maternity Pay

Most working women qualify for Statutory Maternity Pay (SMP). Although funded by the government, such benefit is paid via your employer, through your normal pay channels.

Do I qualify for SMP?

To be entitled to SMP you have to fit the following conditions:

- you were employed by the same employer continuously for at least 26 weeks into the 15th week before the week your baby is due. Loosely translated this means you need to have been with your employer for a minimum of six months by the time you are six months pregnant
- you were earning an average of at least £90 a week (2008/2009) before tax.

To claim SMP you must tell your employer at least 28 days before the date you want to start your maternity leave. Your employer may need you to tell them in writing.

Unless your baby is born sooner, the earliest SMP can start is 11 weeks before the week your baby is due.

How much SMP will I receive?

Pregnant women who meet the qualifying conditions (see above) and who have given the correct notice are entitled to receive up to 39 weeks' SMP.

The rate of SMP is 90 per cent of your average weekly earnings for the first six weeks. For the remaining 33 weeks, you will either receive 90 per cent of your average weekly earnings (as in the first six weeks) or a flat rate of £117.18 (April 2008), whichever is the lower amount.

Contractual (company) Maternity Pay

In addition to SMP your employer might have its own company maternity pay scheme, which would entitle you to more money. Check your contract of employment or

Keeping in touch days

This relatively new initiative encourages women to keep their hand in at work during their maternity leave. Any woman with a child born during or after April 2007 may, by agreement with her employer, complete 10 days' work during her maternity leave. In return, she'll be paid her normal rate and her benefits will be unaffected. It's a great idea to take full advantage of these days if you can; you benefit both financially and professionally. I have completed 10 days work each year I have been on my career break, these are also considered keeping in touch days. I have a few of my keeping in touch days to attend training courses, work from home, read new policies affecting my role and in the office catching up or actually helping with a project. You might find that attending a staff day out or an annual meeting is a useful way of keeping abreast of developments within your workplace. What you do with these days is between you and your employer.

staff handbook, or ask your employer's HR department. All companies are different: I know some company schemes require you to pay back some or all of the contractual maternity pay if you don't come back to work after your specified leave, so check any clauses or conditions that may be attached to this pay. I worked out that if I didn't return to work at the end of my career break for at least 3 months I would owe about £3,500. That's hefty!

Scrutinise your contract in detail to ensure you are getting your full entitlement. A woman in her 20s or 30s yet to have children may want to consider whether to take a job that offers no contractual maternity pay. Managing purely on SMP can be done but can be tricky.

How much CMP will I receive?

How much contractual maternity pay you receive depends entirely on your employer. After the initial period of 90 per cent of my wages for the first six weeks, I then received half my normal pay plus SMP for 12 weeks. After those three months, I received just SMP for the remaining three months. It does vary.

Maternity Allowance

If you can't get SMP from your employer, you might be entitled to Maternity Allowance (MA) instead if you fulfil any of the following criteria:

- you are employed but don't meet the qualifying conditions for SMP (see page 29)
- you are self-employed and pay National Insurance contributions
- you have a Small Earnings Exception certificate (that is, you are self-employed but don't earn enough to pay National Insurance contributions)
- you are not employed but have worked just before or during your pregnancy.

If you fit one of the above, then you will receive MA if:

- you worked (either employed or self-employed) for at least 26 weeks (six months) of the 66 weeks (15 months) before your baby is due
- you earned an average of £30 per week over any 13 of those 66 weeks.

How much MA will I receive?

The standard rate of MA is £117.18 or 90 per cent of your average weekly earnings, whichever is less. You will receive MA for up to 39 weeks (roughly nine months) and it is not liable for income tax or National Insurance contributions.

Child Tax Credit

Families with children can claim Child Tax Credit (CTC) if their income is no more than £58,175 a year (up to £66,350 if you have a child under one). The regular monthly payments you receive will depend upon your annual (joint) income and the age of any children.

The payment is made up of two elements:

- a family element paid to any family with at least one child and worth up to £545 (2008/2009)
- a child element paid for each child in the family and worth up to £2,085 (2008/2009).

You may receive more if you care for a child under one or a disabled child.

Working Tax Credit

If either you or your partner works you may be eligible for Working Tax Credit (WTC). This tax credit includes childcare provision to help families who are working and spending money on childcare.

The idea behind WTC is to top up the earnings of lower-paid workers (whether employed or self-employed). You don't need to have children to qualify and need to earn jointly under £17,500.

How much tax credit will I receive?

Tax credits are based on your household income and individual circumstances, so you'll need to give information that includes:

- your income in the last tax year and the number of hours you normally work a week
- the income in the last tax year of your partner or civil partner (if you have one) and the number of hours he or she normally works a week
- any benefits you're getting
- the number and ages of children (if you have any)
- the amount you spend each week on eligible (that is, registered or approved) childcare.

Child Benefit

Anyone bringing up a child is entitled to Child Benefit. As of January 2009, Child Benefit is £20 per week for your eldest or only child and £13.20 per week for any additional children. It's paid monthly into the nominated parent's bank account. It isn't affected by income or savings, anyone bringing up a child can get it.

Don't miss out on any payments and apply for Child Benefit as soon as you can after your baby is born. Be aware that HM Revenue & Customs can backdate your Child Benefit only for up to three months from the date they get your claim. So, don't delay or you'll lose money.

You should find a claim form in the Bounty Pack that's given to new mums; if not, either go online to www.hmrc. gov.uk/childbenefit/forms.htm to download and print a copy or call the Child Benefit Helpline (0845 302 1444, open 8am to 8pm every day) to order a paper copy. Send your completed form to the Child Benefit Office along with your child's birth or adoption certificate. You cannot claim over the phone or via the Internet.

Child Trust Fund Vouchers

Children born on or after September 2002 are entitled to a Child Trust Fund Voucher of £250. As well as the Child Trust Fund Voucher, children in families with lower incomes will receive an additional payment from the government. Once you have claimed Child Benefit for your child, the voucher will be sent to you automatically.

There are myriad options and banks and building societies vying for your Child Trust Fund Voucher, so investigate the possibilities before deciding which is best for you. The government's own website is worth a look – www.childtrustfund.gov.uk. You, your family and friends can top-up the fund by up to £1,200 a year in total. Only your child will have access to this fund when they reach 18. It is great way to kickstart their savings.

Maternity Exemption Certificate (Matex)

The Maternity Exemption Certificate (otherwise known as Matex) is worth a lot of money if you use it wisely. It is viable all through your pregnancy and up to a year afterwards. By using this exemption form you get free NHS prescriptions and NHS dental treatment.

Applying for benefits

You can apply for most but not all benefits online; others can be done on the phone or via the post. Sometimes it's much easier to discuss a situation with someone on the telephone or in a face-to-face rather than work out benefits online. Benefit phone lines are open long hours and I've always found the staff very helpful. When pregnant with my second child I applied for Maternity Allowance as I had been self-employed during the previous year, the forms were so complicated they made me cry! After just one phone call I knew exactly what to do and the lady on the phone had cheered me up no end by saying everyone found the forms impossible, not just me!

The website that may address your, no doubt, many questions is www.hmrc.gov.uk.

To take full advantage, make sure you complete the application form. (Form FW8 is available from doctors, midwives and health visitors. Ask your health professional to sign to confirm the information given by you is correct. They will then send it off on your behalf.) So, in a nutshell all you need to do is get hold of a form and fill it in. Do use the certificate, don't just store it away and forget about it. It has saved me a fortune, particularly in dental treatment

See the Resource Bank (page 246) for specific contact details.

4. SAVE UP FOR THOSE BABY DAYS

Whether interest rates are high or low, any savings you can make will give your baby fund a boost. If you can, save up ahead of your time off with your baby. Start as soon as you can...it is the best investment you will ever make. Living on less, while you save, is good practice for when it becomes a necessity. Take a good look around on the high street and on the Internet before finding a savings account which suits you; the Saturday supplements have good comparisons on all savings accounts and the best interest rates you can find.

In addition to your soon-to-be regular savings, here are five good ways to boost your fund.

DIRTY NOTES PLEASE – Ask for cash at birthdays and Christmas, as soon as you even start planning your baby and stash it away.

EVERY PENNY COUNTS – Putting away your change at the end of the day into a jar or pot can add up surprisingly quickly. If you're off alcohol during your pregnancy and while breastfeeding, then pop the equivalent of what you'd be spending in the pot. Our penny jar coughed up £90 when we were just desperate for a nappy and baby food shop. We were so glad we had saved that change.

REGULARLY REDIRECT – Instead of cancelling a direct debit, simply redirect the same amount to your savings account. Just a few pounds a week can mount up fast and boost your savings pot – you probably won't even miss it.

THE THREE RS – Reduce, reuse and recycle to lower your energy, food and even clothes shopping bills. For example, as well as getting into the habit of switching things off (not leaving on standby), take a shower instead of a bath where you can. Cut down on food wastage (and so cut down on grocery bills) by being inventive with leftovers – toss scraps of salad into a toasted pitta for a quick snack and wrap that half-eaten baguette from lunch in foil for supper.

WATCH YOUR FUND GROW – It is a good exercise to work out at the end of each day what you think you've saved by being savvy and to put this money into a little box… at the end of a week adding this up will both surprise and inspire you. Any little saving should make you feel virtuous rather than deprived. Even if you just spend what you've squirrelled away on stocking up on baby items, the savings you have made will make a real difference.

5. MAKE YOUR MORTGAGE WORK FOR YOU

Probably the biggest expenditure you have is a mortgage. We made use of our mortgage to free up some money. Consider any of these mortgage options for helping you set up that all-important baby fund.

TAKE A MORTGAGE BREAK – We took a six-month mortgage break and paid nothing during that time. Our bank agreed readily and added the six months on to the end of our mortgage life. This payment holiday gave us some free cash, just when we needed it. Most mortgage providers will consider some kind of mortgage holiday.

SWITCH MORTGAGE TYPES – Our next step was to change from a repayment to an interest-only mortgage. It's only for a maximum of five years until our children go to school. In the short term it has saved us about £200 a month. A warning, though, that when those five years are up, you should either switch back to a repayment type or set up a vehicle to repay the capital of your interest-only mortgage – otherwise you may be paying a mortgage till you're 80!

RELEASE SOME MONEY FROM YOUR MORTGAGE – Remortgaging is another possibility to release a lump sum or lower your monthly mortgage payments if you extend your mortgage term. According to the website www.moneysavingexpert.com: remortgaging involves closing your existing mortgage and opening a new one, with better terms. Usually people remortgage in order to secure lower monthly repayments. It could make sense to help you through the next few years. Again, have a look at the price-comparison sites and talk to your current mortgage lender about your options.

GET A BETTER DEAL – Shop around for a good mortgage rate. If you don't want to trawl round the banks just look online at sites such as www.moneyexpert.com or www.moneysupermarket.com, both of which will provide you with various mortgages. Filling in a form just once could save time and money.

DOWNSIZE – Whether it's moving to a different area or just to a smaller house, a mobile home, caravan or even tent, you could reduce the size of your mortgage by downsizing. We considered them all (except for the tent, that is); it is not forever and a less-expensive property may be just the thing to save on your monthly payments or release a chunk of cash. Do think about schools and friends, though…it is not always so easy to buy back into an area. Another option could be to move closer to grandparents who may be willing to help out with childcare.

Without making our mortgage work for us I could probably not have had my extensive time off work. So, explore the possibilities and don't be afraid to make some positive changes. Bear in mind that these are short-term solutions and mortgages can be topped up or reassessed later should you wish to.

See the Resource Bank (page 270) for some useful details.

6. IS YOUR CAR EASY ON YOUR POCKET?

Cars can be really useful when you have a baby, and I am not suggesting you ditch your car unless you have to. However, you need to future proof yourself when it comes to your choice of car and how you use and abuse it. Consider your car's petrol consumption, boot size, economy and its green credentials: Is it a suitable family car (that is, can you fit a normal buggy in the boot)? Is it economical to run and service? What insurance bracket does it fall into? Can you afford recovery service if it breaks down? Such prompts may well make you swap your four-wheel drive or stylish moped for something more practical and cost effective.

KEEP PAYMENTS LOW – If you're buying a new or second-hand car, find the finance that gives you low monthly repayments or, if possible, pay it all off in one go.

ESSENTIAL CAR MAINTENANCE – You need to be able to keep your car in good, safe condition without resorting to manufacturer's service agreements and costly repairs. Ask around for local garage recommendations (two or three at least) and then ask for quotes before deciding who to use.

SMART BUT SIMPLE – Keep your feet on the ground. You don't need a car that is too smart for the job of family car; it'll soon be plastered with mushed up rice cakes, biscuits and squashed banana, so it's good if the interior is washable, at least.

WALK OR CYCLE WHEN YOU CAN – Fresh air and exercise are fantastic for you, your baby and the environment so walk or cycle when you can and give your car a rest. Your car will thank you in lower wear-and-tear repairs and in keeping petrol costs down.

KEEP AN EYE ON PETROL PRICES – Supermarkets often offer cheap petrol and it is well worth shopping around (within a certain distance) for the best price available. There's a really handy website (www.petrolprices.com) to help you find the lowest UK petrol price in your area. It considers nearly 10,000 petrol stations and has 8,000 daily updates!

DIY VALETING – Washing your own car saves money and gives you a workout; those biceps and triceps will be toned before you know it. Make sure you can get the vacuum cleaner to the car (get a long extension lead) as you'll soon be needing to hoover on a more regular basis and you don't want to have to pay for it.

SHOP AROUND FOR INSURANCE – Get the best deal on your car insurance by shopping around and checking out competing prices through websites such as www.gocompare.com, which is a completely free service with no hidden costs. Women drivers are generally considered safer than men and companies such as Sheila's Wheels and Ladybird cater exclusively for women and offer very competitive insurance premiums. Where possible buy online as quite a few insurance companies offer online discounts.

See the Resource Bank (page 270) for further details.

7. GET YOUR FAMILY AND FRIENDS ON BOARD

Tell your family and friends what you are planning to do about economising and having time off with your baby over the next few years. It is better to prepare them, and involve them if possible, so they may be more considerate regarding any gifts or support they may give to you. You also don't want them to think you are stingy when you no longer buy them expensive gifts or take them out for dinner!

Announce your plans to take time off with your baby and state it with pride and as a matter of fact; don't ask for or expect approval. Don't be embarrassed about being financially constrained either, you are prioritising your child over your career and they will see far more of your baby as a result.

Every week I go to see my children's GG (Great Grandma) and they see their Gran and Grandma at least once a week, too – neither of which would happen if I worked all week, because our weekends would be too precious to us as a small family unit and would be the only time we would have together. My extended family support me in many varied ways. They help me with childcare, playgroup costs, nappy buying, activity fees and organising birthday parties. They know the children incredibly well and consequently they get a great deal of pleasure from watching them grow up and taking part in their development. My mum introduced Frankie to the alphabet, GG helped him to grow tomatoes, Gran has taught him to make green dinosaur biscuits with lots of jam – important life lessons for a five-year-old, as well as a bank of lovely memories. Now his baby sister is here they are all delighted they will be around to watch her grow up, too. We do know how lucky we are to live so close, and I know that if I worked full-time, these visits would be far less frequent.

If you are lucky enough to have family and friends close by, involve them all you can in your baby's life. As the ancient African proverb says, 'It takes a village to raise a child'. If you share your plans, and the reason behind them, you are much more likely to receive greater empathy and more practical support. You may also get some unprompted financial help. My in-laws, for instance, make a small regular monthly contribution towards our living costs as they understand and support what we are trying to do, and this has been invaluable. Other family members and friends have also generously helped us out on numerous occasions.

8. BREAK OPEN THE PIGGY BANK

If you have any savings perhaps now is the time to ask yourself quite what are you saving for? There will never ever be anything more worthwhile spending your savings on than time with your children. Even if you don't go back to work till they start school you still have years to work towards saving them a nest egg for university, buying them a car and helping them with their first house/ wedding/child. But you only have until they are five before they start to build a world away from you. Enjoy them while you can.

I know people who have large savings and rarely see their children as they work so hard (often to save money for their future). Your children are here right now and most children would want mummy or daddy to play with them today rather than a trust fund at 21. (Don't quote me however, as when they reach 21 they may well say they want the trust fund!)

Children grow and build their own little lives in the blink of an eye; those five years go faster than any other in my experience. Of course, we have to look to their future but we have to be with them in the moment. Your baby is your best-ever rainy-day reason for spending your savings.

9. BE MONEY SAVVY

As we said earlier (see page 21), before you bring your little bubba into the world, you need to take stock of your finances. Consider any debts you have before you make any decisions about how much time you can afford to take off work. Unfortunately it can be very easy to get into debt: you go a bit overdrawn or use a credit card and then you get charged interest; you go over on another account to pay it off and you get charged interest; you take out a new credit card to pay off all this interest and so on and so on. Before you know it you are facing real problems.

We are bombarded with TV adverts and mail shots promoting quick fixes to debt problems through yet another loan. Consolidation can be a useful exercise (see page 26) but not if it's become a serial process where you're never really repaying anything, just borrowing more and more and more. Do not buy into any quick fixes. Try very hard to avoid debt in the first place. Don't spend what you haven't got or know is coming in very soon. Pay off credit cards as soon as you can. Only go overdrawn if this is agreed. Talk immediately to your bank if you are in any trouble.

National Debtline (www.nationaldebtline.co.uk) works alongside the government. This charity provides free, independent advice around debt and can offer real support. Explore all such avenues before your problems get serious. Do not bury your head in the sand. You could lose family, friends and even your home. It goes without saying money borrowed needs repaying at some point. Your local Citizens Advice Bureau could also be a useful lifeline either face-to-face, by phone or online. The key is to do something, otherwise your situation will only get worse.

Find more places of support for debt in the Resource Bank (page 249).

CHAPTER 2

Practical Preparations

Before you start buying baby equipment and outfits like there's no tomorrow, stop and consider how you can prepare for your little one's arrival on a budget. There are plenty of easy-on-the-purse options, so you can feel totally prepared and not overwhelmed by all the things you want to sort out before your baby comes.

10. BASIC ECONOMISING

One of the main ways to afford more time off work to be with your baby is to cut back on what you spend; there is no way round it. Forget designer perfume and all-inclusive holidays to Acapulco, for a while at least. Retrain your shopping instinct so that you choose own brands where possible, look out for '3 for 2' offers and become friends with those sale rails.

The reality of budgeting is boring, but that doesn't mean you have to feel bored; accept the challenge of staying within your budget, stay focussed and congratulate yourself when you've succeeded. Remind yourself why you are tightening the purse strings: more time off with your precious baby. Sometimes people just don't get it; I know someone who spent £2,000 on a sofa but moans constantly that she never sees her kids. She works full-time plus overtime and occasionally weekends, too. I'm sure she would be happier revisiting her priorities and cutting down on work but spending more time with her family, but it's not always quite so easy.

Fact: if you want exactly the same lifestyle and spending power that you had before you had children then you probably won't get much time to spend with them. Some things have to change; you don't have to do without but you will have to do things differently.

Basic economising is nothing new and it's not rocket science either. In a nutshell, be smart, organised, creative, share, borrow, lend, buy second-hand and shop around. Your reward for improving your economising skills is a little friend who you can spend hours laughing with, loving, teaching, exploring and growing with. Truly days with your kids will be the best days of your life.

Ask any older female relative for ideas and advice, particularly those who lived through the war, they are often (they had to be) incredibly resourceful. For example, GG (Great Grandma) freezes her bread and takes out just what she needs each morning. One loaf lasts her ages. I should have thought of it myself, but hey, I have been single-handedly keeping the local ducks well fed for years! Common sense and simple ideas are often the winners, so share any successes you have.

11. THRIFTY FOOD SHOPPING

There's one outlay that you can't live without and that's food. But you can reduce this expense by careful planning, smart shopping and getting into good shopping habits before your baby comes along.

Don't waste it

According to the website www.lovefoodhatewaste.com, in the UK on average we throw out about one-third of all the food we buy – approximately £420 worth of food per family per year. Just think what you could do with that! You don't want to waste food, but do pay attention to basic food safety and hygiene. If you realise that a food is going to go out of date before you're going to use it, pop it in the freezer for another time. Any food past its use-by date should be thrown away. Best-before dates are different: they refer to food being in its prime before these dates but still edible though past its best after these dates. Understand food labelling better by checking out www.eatwell.gov.uk.

Write a shopping list

Bare cupboards and last-minute takeaways probably need to be a thing of the past. By planning a weekly menu and writing a shopping list you'll have all you need to make quick, easy and scrumptious meals. You can even factor in low-cost treats: a deluxe pizza is far cheaper bought from a supermarket than ordered in but it still requires minimal effort and hardly any washing up. Result.

My top foodie tips

Ask around for friends' and family members' food shopping and storage tips. Here are just a few of mine.

○ Keep apples in the fridge, they last longer.

○ Store bananas away from other fruit to stop them spoiling.

○ Remove those plastic containers at the bottom of your fridge and replace with airtight boxes to keep salad and vegetables fresher.

○ Use pegs to close cereal packets to stop the contents from going soft.

○ Always store new food at the back of your cupboards; the old gets shunted forwards and will be used well before it's out of date.

○ Store like foods together, then you can see at a glance when you are about to run out of something and replace it.

○ Make your own cakes and biscuits. It takes much less time than you think, can be fun and really is much less expensive than buying them.

○ Always keep your cheese in an airtight container

○ Buy online and in bulk for items you use regularly; try wholesalers and you may get some great deals.

○ Don't get sucked into multibuys unless you will definitely use them.

When to shop, when *not* to shop and when to 'virtual shop'

Before your baby is born you can shop as and when you like, so choose your trolley times wisely and you can pick up some real bargains. Reductions usually begin at 50 per cent around 5pm and go as high as 75 per cent off by 9pm. Ask the staff at your local supermarket what time they do their reductions.

It's obvious but I'll say it anyway – try to avoid shopping when you are hungry. Shopping while your tummy is rumbling is bad for you and bad for your budget; you may well splurge on lots of food (comforting and instantly reviving foods – you know the sort) you don't really need. Even if you've got your list but are feeling a bit low or fed up, ask your partner to go or delay it for tomorrow, otherwise you'll discover that several chocolate cakes and bottles of wine have mysteriously appeared in your trolley.

Shopping online with your regular supermarket or any others can be great for sticking to a list and to a budget. Once you've booked your delivery slot and got the hang of the way the website works, you'll find you can do a weekly shop in about 20 minutes – saving time and, no doubt, saving money. You'll still see special offers and some supermarkets even tailor offers to products that you buy often.

Learn to love your leftovers

Be creative with leftovers; have them the next day for lunch or whiz them up in a blender for a baby puree. There is a real trend towards reducing food waste and food bills in our current economic climate, so make friends with one or more of the following books:

Kate Colquhoun, *The Thrifty Cookbook: 476 ways to eat well with leftovers* (London, Bloomsbury, 2009).

Pamela Le Bailly, *Second Time Around: Ideas and recipes for leftovers*(Oxford, Trafford Publishing, 2007).

Rosie Sykes, Polly Russell and Zoe Heron, *The Kitchen Revolution: Change the way you cook and eat forever – and save time, effort, money and food* (London, Ebury, 2008).

12. STOCK UP AND SAVE

Buying some baby items in advance can be tremendously helpful to spread the cost. Of course, you can't buy every nappy you'll ever need but these are some items that I popped in my supermarket trolley long before my baby came along:

- cotton wool
- nappies
- nappy bags
- baby wipes (fragrance free)
- nappy cream
- baby toiletries (fragrance free)
- plain white sleepsuits
- baby vests
- muslins

- Calpol
- teething rings
- baby nail scissors

While I was pregnant, and working, a few extra pounds spent here or there were hardly noticed. Later on, I was so glad I had stocked up. It's probably not worth filling your cupboards until you're well into your second trimester, and just buy a few bits each time you shop.

If you pre-buy clothes (and it is so tempting!) keep things neutral. Remind yourself that you will receive lots of newborn baby clothes as gifts. It's later on that the clothes supply dries up. Too much advance clothes buying, however, is not always a smart move. My son weighed only 3lb at birth so the summer clothes for a 9lb baby that I had bought were of no use until winter. My advice would be to wait and see what size your little bundle is and buy accordingly – they'll look mighty odd in snowsuits in June!

One thing you could buy in advance and in bulk (if you have the cupboard space) is washing powder suitable for babies. By that, I mean non-biological and fragrance-free; for such little things, babies can get through lots of outfits in one day.

While you're off at the beginning of your maternity leave, you could put a few days aside to do some batch cooking and fill up the freezer with meals that can be easily defrosted and cooked. You may not feel like cooking meals from scratch with a newborn demanding all of your attention plus you'll be far too busy staring at their gorgeous tiny toes!

13. GET THE GIFTS YOU WANT AND NEED

If family and friends ask you if they can buy a gift for your baby, don't be polite and vague, be ready. Have a list of things you want, even with the model number if you're particular, along with each item's approximate cost. A gift of a £500 pram is generous but when you have seen just the one you want for £150 in a second-hand shop, just think of all the other things you could have bought – a cot, Moses basket, bedding, wardrobe and changing table – with the rest of that £500; it's enough to break your money-saving heart!

As this is your gift, your family and friends should be pleased to be able to give you what you want, plus they'll probably be proud of your organisational skills, too. Do ask for specifics – the car sunshade, an expressing machine or baby monitors – otherwise you will find nearly everyone buys clothes. People do like to get you something useful and won't mind a bit that you've made a suggestion. If they do mind, then they really shouldn't have asked should they?

Asking for vouchers is another possibility that often goes down better than asking for money. If you like, you can set up a baby gift list, based on your wish list, at one of many high-street shops much as people do for a wedding. Check out the Resource Bank (page 251) for shops that have this service.

14. VALUABLE VOUCHER CODES

Voucher codes are a brilliant way to save money.

Sometimes known as promotional or discount codes, these special codes will bring you a discount at a variety of online UK retailers as well as some on the high street.

All you have to do is visit one of the voucher code websites, see which store you fancy shopping at and see what discount is offered. You then just note down the relevant code and enter it at the checkout stage when you have finished shopping. Brilliant. Featured stores include Boden, Amazon, Blooming Marvellous, M&S, Dixons and Body Shop. If you're going to make a purchase, it is worth checking out some voucher code sites beforehand.

Refer to the Resource Bank (page 272) for a list of all the voucher code sites I use.

15. TEN GOOD THINGS TO BORROW

Shakespeare wrote 'Neither a lender nor a borrower be' but I don't think he was on a strict budget for kitting out his family. Borrowing is ideal if you are on a tight budget and, equally, lending your equipment or clothes to others will be warmly welcomed. If you are the borrower, look after the items as if they were your own, replace anything you ruin and give them back just as soon as you no longer need them, ideally without having to be asked. And if you do lend, lend with an open heart and do expect some wear and tear, a few scratches, occasional breaks and possibly a few stains. Some baby items can take up valuable storage space when no longer used, so lending them out is ideal for freeing up some room at home. Let the borrower know in advance when you want the item back, perhaps for baby number 2.

From my experience, the following are great baby items to borrow.

A Moses basket

Your baby's first bed is often a Moses basket, which lasts them about four months. Because babies grow so fast these mini-beds get very little wear and tear so are usually in great condition for borrowing. They can easily set you back £50+ new. I borrowed my best friend's gorgeous Moses basket but bought a new mattress as advised by my health visitor. When I gave it back, it still looked pristine and had cost me practically nothing.

A nursing chair

These chairs are pricey but if you've ever sat in one in a nursery department you'll know how comfortable they are. They're brilliant for feeding your baby, they help keep your back straight and you can rock your little one off to sleep in them – and you too if you're lucky. I bought mine on special offer and it has been borrowed twice. It still looks brand new (it does have wipe-clean cushions) and I will sell it on when everyone has finished using it!

Maternity clothes

You still want to look good during your pregnancy but once your normal clothes start to strain at the zips and buttons, it's time to think about some maternity items. Buy as few items as you can and see if friends or sisters can lend you the rest. I have borrowed smart tops, a fantastic pair of jeans and a maternity dress for a wedding (that cost a small fortune, but not by me thankfully.)

Once your baby is born and you gradually reclaim your pre-pregnant wardrobe, return any borrowed items and store any items you bought so that you can lend those out or just keep them for future pregnancies. You may be sick of the sight of them by the end of your pregnancy but I can assure you they will be welcomed back like old friends next time round.

A baby gym

Baby gyms tend to wash and wipe well and seem as if they'd last forever (mine's been in constant use for four years now), and so are ideal items to borrow. If you desperately want a new one put it on your baby wish list (see page 54).

A baby sling

Whether you favour a wraparound or clip in version of a baby sling, these papooses are indispensable, simple to use and great when you need to get on when your baby isn't settling. If washable and well looked after, these slings can support baby after baby after baby. So, let the world know you are up for borrowing one and you are sure to be lent one of these.

A travel cot

If you plan to have baby and still spend time away from home, then a travel cot is essential. They can be quite cumbersome objects and take up valuable storage space in a cupboard so borrowing one – either as and when you need it or for a couple of years – makes total sense.

A Bumbo seat or bouncy chair

These little baby seats bridge the gap between a baby wanting to sit up (about four months) and being able to do so (roughly 7–10 months). They are durable and pretty much unspoilable, so borrow one in the sure knowledge that you can't ever really wreck it! A friend of mine sold hers for £15 on eBay this summer – about a third of its cost – which is amazing as I had borrowed it for both my children and it still looked brand new.

A door bouncer

Because babies grow and develop so fast, there's only a small window of opportunity for them to bounce away in one of these contraptions. Almost all door bouncers I have seen stay in good condition so ask around if anyone has one you can borrow.

Prams

Prams (as in the lie-down flat versions) are only used for a limited period so tend to be an expensive buy. It is a real bonus if you can borrow a pram for a few months until your baby is ready and happy to sit up and see the world. Yes, you can buy a complete travel system but only having to purchase a buggy will save you a lot of money. Because they are only used for a few months, prams can be borrowed and returned with little wear.

I haven't included pushchairs, highchairs, car seats or cots in the 'good to borrow' list as these tend to be required for a long time and get a lot of wear and tear. You don't want to wear something out or have to hand back a borrowed item half way through your use of it, but if your lender was to have another baby you may have to.

Do ask friends and family about borrowing something if you feel comfortable, and always offer in return to lend to trusted friends. Don't be proud. Time off with your baby can depend on being a tad brave about what your needs are. Goodwill depends on you being generous, too.

16. SECOND-HAND SHOPPING

Buying second-hand can save you a small fortune. It is a good habit to get into, not only because it will stretch your budget, but also because it is better for the environment; it's the ultimate in recycling. Cots and clothes for the early days and, later on, toys as your baby grows and develops are all ideal candidates for buying second-hand. Plus, when you've finished with them, you can sell them on again (see page 60) to release some much-needed cash each time your baby moves on to a new stage. Here are 10 great places to buy second-hand goods for your baby or child.

Car boot sales

You often see baby goods at car boot sales and you can get some cracking bargains. My mum bought us a Mamas & Papas caterpillar rocker for £2 a few years ago in perfect condition from her local car boot sale. Often it is a family just like yours having a clear out, so there are good-quality (even designer) goodies alongside some complete tat. Be discerning and have a good look around. To find your nearest car boot, go to www.carbootjunction.com or look in your local paper.

eBay

The online auction house eBay is very easy to use (I am sure you already know this). It's where buyers and sellers can come together to trade almost anything. A seller lists an item for sale – anything from Grandfather clocks to cot bumpers – and chooses to accept bids for the item (an auction-type listing) and/or to offer the 'Buy It Now' option, which allows buyers to purchase the item right away at a fixed price. The buyer also pays postage.

In an online auction, the bidding opens at whatever price the seller has specified and remains on eBay for a certain number of days. Buyers then place bids on the item. When the listing ends, the buyer with the highest bid wins. In a Buy It Now listing, the first buyer willing to pay the seller's price gets the item. The seller will also specify how you will get the item – via the post or in person (collection only). When bidding on eBay I find it's safest to decide what your maximum price is and put it in about two days before the listing ends. That way, you're not tempted to keep upping the bids; I've seen some items go on eBay second-hand for more than they cost new! Another tip for a winning bid is to use anything but round numbers for your bid: if, for example, I'm bidding on a door bouncer and I've decided that £15 is my limit then I'll put in £15.03 or £15.11 as my maximum bid.

In my experience buying on eBay is easy – you just follow the simple online directions. Type in the title or browse the categories for the item you want and then place a bid. You can pay for items by cheque or banker's draft or even cash on collection, but the safest option is to set up and use a PayPal account.

My best eBay buys have been a Quinny Buzz for £150 (less than half its retail value and it was brand new!) and an angora Monsoon poncho for my baby for £1.50 (completely unnecessary but adorable and almost free).

NCT nearly new sales

The National Childbirth Trust (NCT) is the leading charity for pregnancy, birth and parenting in the UK. No doubt there will be a group close to you and where there is a group you will invariably find a nearly new sale. These events offer very good quality nearly new baby goods from other parents at a fraction of their original cost. Twenty-five per cent of all the proceeds goes to the NCT charity, so you are giving while saving which is always a nice feeling. But do be aware that these sales are popular and you may well have to queue in advance of the opening time to get the best bargains.

I love these events and have bought (and sold) a great deal through them. Look on the website www.nct.org.uk/home and type in your postcode to find your local NCT nearly new sales.

Freecycle

Freecycle (www.freecycle.org) is a fabulous online resource where people literally give their stuff away. As the name suggests, everything advertised on Freecycle must be free – whether it's an old cot, unwanted clothes or even a few baby books. Anyone interested simply replies by email: deal done.

It is just one of a number of websites that could play a valuable part in reducing the amount of rubbish sent to landfill sites by encouraging one of the most efficient forms of recycling – giving things to people who want them. Freecycle is organised into group areas and you can find your local group by typing in your area name and signing up. They don't just have baby stuff on offer, there's all sorts of things. Most items are collected in person as items are passed on within local areas. If items need to be posted, costs can be arranged between individuals.

My friend Nicki almost totally kitted out her baby this way. She is a real greenie and this way of acquiring baby paraphernalia suited her pocket as well as her ethics. Give freecycle a whirl. Remember it too, when you're ready for a clear out or want to pass on any unwanted items that may be too large or too tatty for eBay or a car boot sale.

Charity shops

The key to getting great second-hand stuff is to travel to wealthy areas and visit their charity shops. You will find inexpensive quality items cheaply priced plus you will be supporting a good cause at the same time. It's a win–win situation.

Don't discount an item that needs attention. You can get simple alterations done at the dry cleaners, if you can't do it, and a broken zip is easily fixed. It would be a shame to pass on that wonderful old rocking horse that needs a little tlc, but then don't take on anything too major – it might become a permanent feature in your garage or garden.

Classifieds

There is often a classified section in your local newspaper for second-hand baby items so ask your local newsagent which day this section appears and be sure to give it the once over. Be safe though: if you arrange to view an item, take someone with you.

Shop windows and noticeboards

Post offices, supermarkets, shop windows or child-friendly cafés often have noticeboards where you can sell items you no longer need, particularly those too heavy to post. Do a bit of local window-shopping and see what is advertised near you. I have often seen prams and cots sold this way; in fact I sold a Moses basket this way. I took a photo and attached it to some card with a description and set off to a local café where lots of mums meet. My notice didn't even make the noticeboard as one of the waitresses (who was pregnant) bought it straightaway.

Friends

If you have a friend who has some great baby stuff and you know she is looking to sell it on why not offer to buy it? You would know it's from a clean home and has been well taken care of, plus you may get a good price. But, it's sometimes tricky with friends; you don't want to get into the situation where your friend thinks he or she should just give it to you. If you know they were going to sell it, insist you pay for it, don't let it affect your friendship. Do be aware that if an item from a friend turns out to be faulty it's not that easy to complain or take it back.

Specific mum and baby websites

The Internet is a godsend when you need to source a specific second-hand item, and there are plenty of second-hand sale sites. As well as checking out the websites below, just type whatever it is you're after into a search engine (such as www.google.co.uk) along with the words 'second hand' or 'nearly new' and hey presto! A list at your fingertips to browse through.

Here are few useful sites I've used, but the list could go on and on.

Mothers2b (www.mothers2b.co.uk) sells second-hand maternity clothes and is well worth a look.

My mummy and me (www.mymummyandme.co.uk) sells second-hand feeding equipment and bath stuff, baby clothes and toys.

Early Baby (www.earlybaby.co.uk) sells nearly new clothes for premature babies – an invaluable site as these items can be hard to find.

Jumble/tabletop sales

Local schools, church halls and community centres often have jumble sales and tabletop sales and you'll be amazed at how much baby stuff turns up at such events. Your library noticeboard or local paper will publish dates of forthcoming sales, so what are you waiting for? Get those elbows at the ready. Sometimes, it is worth getting there early or even offering to help out, so you can snap up the best bargains.

Check out the Resource Bank (see page 264) for all contact details.

CHAPTER 3

Have a Lovely Pregnancy

Your pregnancy is a special time, and still will be even though you're on a budget. While your body is busy growing your baby, you need to take care of yourself – that means plenty of relaxation and pampering. Make the most of these precious months ahead of your baby's arrival, by indulging yourself and spending quality time with your partner, friends and family; such pleasures needn't cost the earth. You can be sure to enjoy a truly lovely pregnancy without ever feeling overstretched.

17. READ ALL ABOUT IT – BOOKS ON A BUDGET

It is wonderful to read books about pregnancy, birth and beyond, and it's wise to be as informed as possible about the stage of life you are about to enter. There's nothing like having a good reason to put your feet up, especially in those last few weeks of pregnancy, so find yourself a good pregnancy book and see how your baby is developing week by week. Ask friends for their recommendations; some women buy three or four books but only ever end up reading one.

While waiting for your baby's arrival and still earning a regular salary it is easy to fritter away your cash on such reading matter. Do bear in mind that you won't read these books much in the future, and some are expensive to buy. So, rediscover your local library and borrow the titles you want. If you need to keep a book past the usual four-week loan period, most libraries now allow you to renew by phone or online. If you find one that is indispensable, buy yourself a copy second-hand from www.amazon.co.uk or www.abebooks.co.uk; you can always sell it on afterwards. Friends who've been through pregnancy are bound to have books you can borrow, too.

If you haven't been to your local library in a number of years you might well find they have changed a great deal. They open late and at weekends. They have computers so you can look up book locations. Most libraries allow you to reserve a book online and will email or call you when it's ready for collection. My local library will order in a book or CD on request if I pay 50p towards it. Check out yours to see what services it has that you can take advantage of. The best place to start looking is at your local council's website, there should be a section on libraries there. Another advantage of borrowing books is less clutter. Books take up much-needed space and soon you're going to need all the storage space you can get.

See the Resource Bank (page 252).

18. EXERCISE FOR FREE

Consult your doctor or midwife before starting out on any new exercise to ensure it is okay during your pregnancy. Everyone is different and just because you have a friend who jogs while pregnant doesn't mean it's going to be the best thing for you.

Since you've now possibly ditched your gym membership, here's how to exercise during pregnancy without breaking the bank.

LACE UP THOSE TRAINERS AND GO – Walking is cheap and the fresh air is fantastic for you and your growing baby. Enhance your activity by choosing a beautiful location, and always choose to go during daylight (do keep safe). Don't stray off the beaten track, especially in those final weeks of pregnancy, but it is good to have time alone to think, plan and dream. Walks with friends are great to chat over anxieties and hopes, and share the excitement of what's just around the corner. Opting for an evening walk with your partner instead of a meal out at a restaurant will keep you both fit and active – plus you'll save the price of a meal. Time out of the house as a couple can help you feel relaxed and make it easier to think and talk about how your lives are soon to change.

A WATERY WORKOUT – Swimming is fantastic exercise throughout your pregnancy, and when done at local pools is a cheap and cheerful exercise option, much less pricey than the gym membership that never gets used. The water supports your ever-growing bump and so if you're feeling heavy then swimming is a great antidote – though, sadly, you will have to get out of the pool at some stage and sometimes that can feel hard.

IN THE COMFORT OF YOUR OWN HOME – Exercise DVDs designed for pregnancy can be far cheaper than classes, but only if you actually do the exercises at home – just having them sit on the shelf under the TV isn't enough! Whether you choose yoga, pilates or aerobics, all such programmes can be done in the warmth and comfort of your own front room when you feel like it, not when they are timetabled. It's also good to know they are totally safe for pregnant women. I borrowed a pregnancy yoga video from my sister-in-law who had, in turn, borrowed it from a friend. So, that's zero cost and always available. Perfect.

ANTENATAL ANTICS – If you are more of an exercise class girl, then choose one specifically designed for pregnant women. Exercising with others can be fun and offers an opportunity to make some friends who are in the same boat. The list of classes is long but popular ones include aquanatal, pregnancy yoga, pilates for pregnancy and antenatal fitness.

19. THAT'S WHAT FRIENDS ARE FOR

Making new mummy friends whose bumps are at about the same stage as yours is vital for your sanity, your future baby's social life and for your budget. When your bump starts to show (let's face it, you'll be pushing it out a bit initially), you'll find you notice other women's bumps too. And with trips to the midwife and parenting classes there will be ever-more opportunities to meet people going through the same thing.

Netmums (www.netmums.co.uk) have 'meet a mum' noticeboards where you can post your details and hook up with like-minded mums in your local area. Six out of 10 mums surveyed by netmums said they wanted new friends and around 1,000 links a month are made nationwide. (As always on the Internet do stay safe, and don't leave details of your child's school or post photos till you have met up; and do meet up in a public place.)

A class act

Parenting classes at the local health centre or at the hospital are perfect times to meet other mums and dads. You'll be offered the free NHS antenatal classes and some people opt for the paid-for NCT-run classes too (see page 72). I found the NHS classes allayed any fears and helped me plan ahead. It's good to make an effort to get to know others who live near to you but you have to have something more in common than a bump, you have to be on a similar wavelength too. When the class finishes, why not suggest a coffee back at yours or a walk around the park? I guarantee there'll be plenty of other mums desperately keen to be your friend and eager to meet up too. This community of women you are about to join is invaluable: you can share tips, talk about any pregnancy concerns and help you while away those last few weeks of maternity leave without you hitting the shops. I have always been the one to initiate the coffee or walk, and I am so glad I did. Five years on I still have a network of very good friends made at that time.

Share and share alike

Having mum friends can save you a fortune. My antenatal friends and I have shared toys, clothes, books, lunches and budgeting advice. We have given each other lifts, free counselling sessions and lots of cups of tea and changes of scenery – avoiding the need for playcentres and cafés to entertain our little ones. I even know friends who shared their TENS machine and birthing ball costs, being due just one month apart. Antenatal friends can be friends for life, and this is priceless.

Think like a couple

If you can, get your partner to go along to the classes, too, it gets them up to speed of what to expect in the not-too-distant future and you may make some couples friends. Later on, you will find you have so much in common – you will be skint and shattered and you will all be happy to talk about nappies, sleep and treasured 'firsts'. Other parents are usually keen to meet up at a park or round at someone's house, which cuts down many costs on the socialising front.

It's not free but great value for money

If you don't want to go to your local health centre or for some reason they don't offer antenatal classes, do contact the

National Childbirth Trust (www.nctpregnancyandbabycare. com). The NCT runs a range of private antenatal classes, bringing together groups of parents who live locally and who are due to give birth around the same time. NCT classes start at about £80 and can rise up to £240. It does sound expensive, but just think in terms of budgeting a weekly cup of tea at a cafe can cost you about £75 a year. Far better you drink your tea while you're learning about what lies ahead; and later on, your tea can be had with friends while your baby plays and you get to relax and chat. It is money well spent.

See the Resource Bank (page 248) for more information.

20. LOOKING GOOD FOR LESS

After your first trimester, you're probably already blooming marvellous. You may be discovering the benefits of pregnancy hormones: thicker, shiny hair, a rosy complexion and great nails. Looking good can make you feel great and it doesn't have to be expensive.

Clothes

Long gone are the days when a smock or a pair of oversized dungarees were the only pregnancy attire – and thank goodness! You still want to look good when you are pregnant but when you're on a budget you can't be breaking the bank on kitting yourself out with a wardrobe of new maternity clothes.

BUY A FEW KEY PIECES – We have talked already about borrowing any bits you can (see page 55). If the clothes you've borrowed don't amount to much, you are best to invest in a few classic maternity pieces, such as jeans with a big, stretchy panel, some stretchy black trousers (for work or the weekend), a simple jersey dress, a couple of going-out tops and then cheap comfy Ts. If you wear a smarter look for work then a cute pinafore dress or a maternity jacket/trouser ensemble should fit the bill. And you can always accessorise to keep your own sense of style – you are more than just a bump.

CHECK OUT THE HIGH STREET – Depending on your body shape, you may be able to get away with buying a size up from the cheaper high-street shops, such as Primark or George – that can save you a fortune. But many high-street names have their own reasonably priced maternity lines; try Top Shop, Next, H&M, New Look and Dorothy Perkins for some trendy maternity clothes. Your fella's big Ts might be great to sleep in and his jeans might well do for a while at least. And remember, our old friend eBay is a great place to look for second-hand maternity items.

MADE TO MEASURE – A resourceful woman I know took her favourite pair of Gap jeans to a tailor and paid just £10 to have the front panel cut out and some black stretchy material sewn in. She wore these until the was seven months pregnant and then again after the baby was born. These looked loads better than any she had tried on in the shops and were the right length and cut for her. What a great idea!

PLAN AHEAD – You will be wearing maternity clothes for a little while after the birth, too. I needed my maternity clothes for a good few months post-baby, particularly the tops when I was breastfeeding. When choosing your maternity tops, bear in mind that soon you'll be needing access to your baby's milk supply so tops that access through the front, with a zip or buttons, are the way to go.

DIY beauty

Fact: if you look good you tend to feel good. If you want to go down the earth mother route that's fine but if you wore make-up and got your nails done before you were pregnant then you'll want to keep this up during your pregnancy. Your hair will, no doubt, be looking fabulous but keep an eye on its condition and get it cut regularly. Manicures can be hard to do yourself, so invite a friend round and do each others – it's cheaper and you get to catch up at the same time. If in the early days of your pregnancy, you're feeling peaky and a bit pale, then dig out your bronzer to pep yourself up and boost your confidence. Perfume can be a great final touch as you leave the house, but it can make some women feel nauseous, so do try it out first.

Do you have a friend who's a hairdresser? You could make huge savings if a friend could trim or colour your hair for you. If not, then switch from your salon to a mobile hairdresser who visits you in the comfort of your own home and costs you much less. Now's the time to ask around. I saved myself £30 a cut/colour by going off the high street and my hair looks just as good (see page 159).

The right kind of support

Underwired bras can soon become uncomfortable as your body changes shape and size during pregnancy. It may be as early as the end of your first trimester that you want to find a softer, supportive alternative. Visit the lingerie department in a department store or a high-street shop, such as M&S. You should have expert fitting and buy two or three bras.

If you're planning to breastfeed your baby, you will need a few nursing bras but do not waste money buying one too early. Wait until the very end of your pregnancy, or even after your milk's come in (you can wear a supportive vest till then), as your size and shape can change dramatically.

21. KINDNESS COSTS NOTHING – TAKE CARE OF YOURSELF

Pampering isn't essential to a healthy pregnancy; millions of women around the world don't ever pamper their pregnancies. But living in the West exposes us to ever more sophisticated marketing campaigns and products that you're made to feel you must buy. Don't buy into it! Keep your cash to extend your play times with your baby, and instead of buying 'specially designed for mums-to-be' products and luxurious lotions and potions, just be very kind to yourself. Do you need to spend £40 on anti-stretchmark oil (it exists I assure you)? What you do need to do is take good care of yourself in simple and inexpensive ways.

- Relax every day for 20 minutes (whether that's during a long bath or listening to music)
- Moisturise well
- Drink plenty of fluids
- Eat a varied and healthy diet
- Keep active for fitness and flexibility
- Laugh and sing whenever you can
- Put your feet up, whenever you get the chance, to rest your legs
- Get out in the fresh air
- Have early nights if you need to
- Talk out your stresses and strains with your nearest and dearest
- Get a lovely massage from someone close
- Let someone you love wash or brush your hair for you
- Place cucumber slices or cold teabags on tired eyes.
- Chill out and take a nap if you have a headache or are just shattered
- See your doctor if you feel worn out

No amount of expensive lotions and potions can beat the above for a healthy, glowing pregnancy. Find out what works for you. It can be relaxing just to have your feet rubbed or to stroke your cat, you don't need to buy 'stuff' to bring you peace.

Taking care of yourself costs more in terms of effort than money but it really can change how you feel – and tell yourself, you are worth it.

A special treat

Many spas give pregnant women a great discount, which is often not advertised. There are, of course, things you can't take advantage of during pregnancy (steam rooms and saunas, for example) but there are plenty of other treats instead. On a recent family trip to Center Parcs, I was 15 weeks pregnant and had a three-hour session in their fantastic spa for just under £10 instead of £35. What a bargain; it was a complete treat and left me feeling fantastic.

See the Resource Bank (page 271) for more information.

22. EAT WELL WITHOUT EATING INTO YOUR SAVINGS

Your body needs a varied and nutritious diet to be able to grow a baby and to fuel your day-to-day life. Your midwife, doctor or healthcare provider will be able to give you some basic nutritional advice. When shopping, buy fresh and local where possible but don't go mad: a simple, well-balanced diet is the order of the day.

A MENU PLANNER – Planning your meals for the week means you'll never have to scrabble round in your food cupboards and create some weird and wonderful concoction or phone for a takeaway. By planning meals you will have in exactly what you need.

THE MOST IMPORTANT MEAL OF THE DAY – Eating cereal (the non-sugary kind) for breakfast is delicious and relatively cheap. It is quick to prepare and always at hand, packed with all your essential vitamin and minerals and not too calorific. Perfect! Stock up when you see any special offers.

SOMETHING SPECIAL – Every so often make an occasion of your meals; use a tablecloth, your good plates, and add a little bunch of flowers. This way you will feel you are eating like a queen even if it's beans on toast!

REACH FOR THE WATER – It is not only good for you and your baby to give up coffee and avoid alcohol, it is also good for your purse. Instead, quench your thirst with water – you will have tons more energy.

PURSE-FRIENDLY LUNCHES – Instead of lunching out in restaurants and cafés, especially in those 'I'm a lady who lunches' days towards the end of your pregnancy, take a picnic to the park or enjoy a sandwich on a bench with a friend. As well as being sociable and inexpensive, you get some lovely fresh air too.

BYO SUPPERS – Have a dinner party where friends each bring a dish, so you're not providing all three courses. You will save lots of money and it'll be fun!

DELEGATE THE COOKING – If you are too tired and pregnant to cook then don't. Ask your partner to make dinner tonight; the menu plan is done already so you should have all the ingredients you need.

COLOURFUL INSPIRATION – A stroll around a fruit and veg market is not only a great way to pass the time, you can pick up some great food bargains too.

23. MAKING THE MOST OF BABY-FREE DAYS

You and your partner are about to embark on a brand new life chapter; one in which there won't be the same amount of time for just the two of you. So, try out some of the ideas below for some romance on a budget – and you'll feel good and enjoy the additional boost of not being out of pocket.

- Walking in the park just as the sun goes down.
- Taking a picnic to somewhere beautiful.
- Doing the Orange Wednesday offer at the cinema.
- Enjoying a weekend away at a friend's near the coast.
- Sharing a bag of chips by the river.
- Reading the papers together on a lazy Sunday morning.
- Getting out your photo album and talking through all those wild days of your past/wedding/first date.
- Having a lovely, long bath together (depending how far on in your pregnancy you are, this may be a bit of a squeeze).
- Having friends round for dinner and talking for hours.
- Renting a DVD that you watched together when you first met and snuggling on the sofa.

It's not only partner-time you need to indulge, think about your friends, too. Of course, you'll still see your friends once your baby is born, but these times will be less often so try and make the most of now. Again, these catch-ups don't need to cost anything: you could just share food at your home or theirs and stay up talking as late as you like; you could even have a sleepover! Or get several friends together for a spa day round at your house, with each of your girlfriends bringing a beauty treat along. Gather up your nail varnishes, face packs and hand cream and you can take it in turns to pamper each other and save a fortune on what you would pay at a beautician's.

My friend Sarah had her antenatal friends over one evening late on in their pregnancies to make virgin cocktails – everyone bought something to contribute and they had loads of fun experimenting (even if they did feel slightly sick at the end!). Why not relive your teens and go into town, window shop and gossip. It's loads of fun even if you only spend £2 on a new lipgloss and it won't be the same with a baby in tow.

And for yourself? Lie-ins will soon be a thing of the past (at least for quite a few years), so indulge in them now while you can. Have breakfast in bed at the weekend with lots of good (library) books and some great TV... inexpensive but such a luxury.

24. DON'T WASTE YOUR WAGES ON THE WARD

It's all too easy to overspend on kitting out hospital bags. Probably because it's the one thing we can control in a time of uncertainty and we want to be prepared. It is a fact of life that no one cares a bit what your hospital bag looks like, yet you will invariably devote quite a lot of energy (and money) to making sure it looks good and contains exactly what the books say it should. Some shops sell hospital bags already packed up for you, and these retail at up to £60. You might only be in hospital a day or even not at all (if you are planning a home birth or if baby turns up before you can get to hospital), so stick with just the basics.

I would suggest a biggish bag with three little carrier bags inside for easy access and so you aren't scrabbling around for what you need.

Bag 1 contains things for when you are in labour:

- snacks and drinks (for you and your partner)
- a nightie or big T-shirt (something old and worn is fine; you do not need a maternity nightie, they are very expensive. PJs with buttons down the front are also fab for feeding.)
- a few magazines
- a hair brush (and lippie, if you want, for photos)
- the camera (don't forget this!)
- CDs of your favourite music or iPod with speakers
- basic toiletries, your toothbrush and toothpaste.

Twice I have packed such a birthing bag only to have two Caesareans but, hey, I still used everything I had packed!

Bag 2 is for the baby. I would suggest taking:

- a blanket
- some muslin squares
- a little hat
- some scratch mittens

- two sleepsuits
- two vests
- some nappies

Many supermarkets do cheap 'newborn sets' for very little money. And as I've said before, it is a good idea to buy white – it's cheap, sweet and neutral. Let others buy you some more colourful stuff and there's plenty of time to dress up your little one after.

You will need to take some nappies to the hospital. If you opt for real nappies, choose a size that covers most of the outcomes – the newborn size may well not fit your 11lb bonny boy. Don't assume hospitals will have spare nappies, though you can ask. A bag of disposables in size 1 are a good idea to take in with you. Newborn babies can get through between 8 and 10 nappies a day so I would include just a small pack to see you through a day or two.

Bag 3 inside your hospital bag is for the rest of your stay and should include:

- clothes for you for the next couple of days – do take maternity clothes
- a nursing bra if you plan to breastfeed
- some breast pads
- some sanitary pads and big cheap pants (or disposable maternity pants) not glamorous but oh-so essential. You can lose a lot of blood after giving birth
- toiletries to see you through; no strong scents, baby just wants to smell mum
- your address book and money for the phone or your mobile

These are cheap bags to pack and will see you through. Many hospital bag lists are way longer than this, but as you pack do think are the items really necessary? Anything else can be bought in for you (shops don't close because you have a baby).

Think twice before packing

Do think before you buy any extras. Most people I know never used the following while in hospital:

O an electric fan
O a birthing ball
O nipple creams
O games
O energy sweets
O hot water bottles
O scented candles
O battery operated CD player
O massage oils
O maternity nighties
O your own TV!

CHAPTER 4

Baby's Arrival

You'll have been looking forward to meeting your little one for quite a few months now, and that day is finally here. Once your baby is born, there may seem like a lot of extra things to do in addition to looking after them. So, I'll share with you some practical and creative financial solutions to making savings from the day your baby arrives – from announcing the birth and baby gift lists to thrifty thank-you cards and getting plenty of free help.

25. BUDGET BIRTH ANNOUNCEMENTS

Receiving a birth announcement is lovely; making them or, actually, even just writing them can be quite a task. I had romantic visions of my baby quietly sleeping while I stuck cute little photos on to homemade cards and lovingly wrote out the birth date and weight to all my loved ones. In reality, everyone wanted to know everything straight away. Also the number of people to tell was reminiscent of mega-

Christmas-card lists, and I just did not have the energy for it. Sending cards is also an expensive endeavour.

I thought I had the money-savvy solution when I asked my darling hubby to call everyone straight after the birth to tell them our news. But, he pointed out he had neither the time nor the desire to speak to in excess of 50 people (mainly my friends) straight after our baby's birth and that he would probably head for the nearest pub after calling his mum. In the end I found that the best (and cheapest) solution was threefold:

1. To email a photo with a short message (including those all-important details – birth date, weight, sex, name) and any visiting/contact wishes, to all those you have email addresses for. Emails cost nothing and everyone gets to keep the photo.
2. To send a text message with the details to anyone for whom you don't have an email address.
3. To call one person, pass on all the info and ask them to let x, y and z know and to explain to x, y and z that you are so worn out at the moment you are sorry you didn't get to tell them personally.

If all else fails, ask a female relative (mums and sisters love to help, I know) to call certain people to announce the birth. I really thought I would want to do this myself but when the time came I just wanted to cuddle up with my baby.

Sending photos, unless you do it online, can be expensive. And, in my experience, people tend to take their own photos when they visit; and, let's face it, newborn pics are never the best – worn-out mummies and wrinkly babies are lovely for your memory box but not always to share.

In a few weeks, you may well feel like creating an online album, sending a mass email with photos, or calling or sending texts while feeding your baby (you will soon be expert at multi-tasking). But, for now keep it simple and minimise how much you need to do and how much you spend. No one will mind how they are contacted, just as long as they are.

26. MAKE THE MOST OF THE FREEBIES

While in hospital you will be given a Bounty Pack – a bag full of goodies relating to having a new baby; if you have your baby at home, your midwife will be able to get your pack for you. You will also be able to pick one up from Boots or Asda before or after the birth. Don't just bin these as a frivolous marketing exercise, these little bags are a treasure trove of money-off vouchers and samples.

Use your vouchers to try out all the nappies to see how they fit your baby; there's no shame in being a nappy tart since nappies are all much of a muchness at the newborn stage.

Do get your free photos taken too (I had vouchers for four different photo sessions in my pack) as these make brilliant gifts at Christmas or birthdays and save you a packet.

The samples included in your Bounty Pack vary from time to time but tend to include tiny pots of nappy cream, sachets of washing powder, little bottles of handsoap and a small pack of wipes (sometimes with a box). Such small versions of useful baby toiletries can be handily kept in a nappy changing bag and topped up as and when they need to be. I received my Bounty Pack the day after delivery and felt overwhelmed by all the free stuff it contained. My advice would be to put it to one side for a few weeks and explore it later when you are more up to it. It really is great. Bounty also has a website (www.bounty.com/packs) where they have printable money-off coupons that change every week, so make it a regular site to visit when and if you do manage to get on the computer.

Look out for freebies all the time – on the front of a parenting magazine, for example, or in the nappy aisle at the supermarket. Some nappy manufacturers often have a free nappy-bag promotion, which is well worth getting as a spare. Don't be proud, spend any vouchers you receive and look out for all special offers. Join other baby clubs, such as those run by Boots and Tesco, for instance, which all offer discounts and useful information.

Check the Resource Bank (page 268) to find out more about freebies and how to get them on a regular basis.

27. NEW BABY VISITS – HIDE THE CAKE!

You'll no doubt enjoy showing off your precious bundle to an endless stream of visitors, but don't worry about providing cakes, biscuits and countless pots of tea. Not only will this cost you a fortune but you have bigger priorities at this time, such as resting, feeding and taking care of your baby. Any friends with children who visit will most probably bring their own, plus some extra, make the tea and then do any washing up before they go.

My advice, especially if your partner is not there to

help out, would be to set the coffee, tea and squash out on a tray in the kitchen along with a packet of digestives (unless it's your bestest friend, then bring out the chocolate ones). Then, say to people who visit, 'Feel free to put the kettle on and help yourself to a drink'. Next time they come, they'll probably bring you a more exciting accompaniment to a cuppa – hooray. You certainly don't want to end up out of pocket, and your baby visitors wouldn't want that either.

My friend Giselle never visits a new mum without taking a simple meal of, say, fresh pasta and sauce and some just-cooked, crusty bread. How thoughtful! Make a mental note of any acts of kindness like this so that you can do the same for other mums when they have a new baby in the house.

28. GET THE BABY GIFTS YOU WANT AND NEED

Most people are literally showered with new baby gifts and undoubtedly feel overjoyed so many people care. But, you want to avoid being in the situation where you are given 30 newborn vests, seven dresses and 10 pairs of scratch mitts, all in the same size. That just equals a waste of money. Babies grow so fast and so many items never make it out of the cupboard. Don't let this happen to you.

Return or exchange

You can always take things back to the shop they were purchased from and exchange duplicates for other items you need. If you really hate a gift, it is fine to exchange it; most friends and relatives would rather you have something useful or something that you liked. Nearly all shops allow you to return baby clothes for a refund (with the receipt) or for a credit note without the receipt. You can choose to swap them for something you like or use the credit note towards a larger item, such as a highchair. (I have done this many, many times with clothes given to me. Sssssssssssh.)

The same goes for toys. If you're given the same or similar toys twice then take one back and exchange it for something else. Three identical rattles will be no fun for your baby and seeing as you still have one, who will ever know?

Sell on

Occasionally you may be bought a gift that you're not keen on but that you cannot return. Some shops insist on receipts altogether and some items could be handmade or come without a label. As we've said before (see page 59) and delve into in more detail in Chapter 11 (see page 204), NCT nearly new sales, eBay and car boot sales are great places to sell unwanted items. Any money saved or earned in this way is a bonus, plus your house will be less cluttered. Gifts are always intended to bring pleasure, not sit in a drawer, so this way at least they are of use.

Filling the present drawer

Passing pristine, unwanted or duplicate baby gifts that you cannot return onto others as new baby gifts (regifting) is also a top idea (as long as they didn't give it to you obviously).

Anything too hideous for you may well be too much for someone else, so think twice before passing it on – it will not win you any friends. It's best to drop those items off at the local charity shop or sell them at a car boot sale.

Have a gift list

In Chapter 2 (see page 54), we look at the benefits of a gift list – you get what you want, and everyone knows that whatever's on the list is good so their shopping is easy. So, if someone asks you what you want – tell them. Setting up a baby gift list might make everyone's life easier and will avoid duplicate gifts. See the Resource Bank (page 251) for more details.

29. THRIFTY THANK-YOU CARDS

Now the mountain of gifts have been given, you'll have to get round to those all-important thank-you cards. Saying thank you need cost very little. Buy some blank white postcards, stick on a photo of your baby and write 'thanks for the pressie' beneath it and everyone will be happy. These are cheap, the recipient gets to see your baby and you don't have to remember who bought what, always a bonus. You can have a bunch of these done in an hour or two, stacked and ready to go. You can also post them second-class as there really is no rush.

If you are the creative type, don't have too many cards to do and have a patient and obliging baby, then what could be more cute than printing a baby foot or hand on the front of a plain postcard as your thank-you note? People really appreciate a thank-you card whatever form it arrives in, so just wait until you're feeling recovered and do them as and when, there's no need to stress yourself over thank-you cards.

30. YOUR BABY'S FINANCIAL FUTURE

Investing in your baby is something that your relatives may well want to do. They may bring this up right after the baby's birth. Money put away until your child is 18 is a great idea for the future but it's not such a great idea if, for a couple of years, the same amount would enable you to afford more time at home with your baby. For example, £50 a month for three years is £1800 saved for the future. But while you are off work with your baby, such an amount could pay for food, nappies and a host of baby-centred activities.

It can be tricky talking about money, but be brave. Try to explain what your aims are to your relatives if they want to make regular savings on your baby's behalf. Ask if, just for a limited period, they would mind paying gift money into a current account instead, and then switch to a long-term account when you are back at work. Point out the benefits to your baby of your being at home. This isn't cheeky, it's smart. We did this... It isn't an easy conversation to have but it worked out well for us. There is no harm in asking. My in-laws put money in the bank each month for my children and I draw it out for food and to pay for any activities or trips. This help has been priceless, so it's definitely worth being courageous enough to discuss it.

31. ACCEPTING HELP – FINANCIAL AND PRACTICAL

Learn a new mantra: I will accept all offers of help. It can be hard to let others help you, financially and practically, but now is the time to swallow your pride and do just that. Accept all offers of practical help full stop – whether it's for returning gifts, writing out thank-you cards and birth announcements, buying groceries, cleaning, or ironing from anyone and everyone who offers. This saves all your energy for you and your baby. Do remind yourself that you are recovering from a long pregnancy and the birth of a baby; no doubt, you'll be more sleep-deprived than you had probably ever imagined, so getting others (those with non-sleep-addled brains) to do things for you actually makes sense all round. Financially too, if your mum picks you up some bread and milk and insists on paying, don't argue – accept gratefully and savour the support. If friends offer to treat you to a coffee, say yes and smile; and remember, you will be in a position to treat them soon enough.

Recently, during a particularly tiring week, I looked at my kitchen and saw a massive cleaning job to be done – it was bad, I promise you, which is something since I am not particularly house proud. I just couldn't imagine finding the time to do it. If I could have brought in a cleaning service I would have done so in a heartbeat. So, do you know what I did? I called in my own version of the Merry Maids: Mum and my lovely Aunty Jane. This dynamic duo cleaned my kitchen till it gleamed just because I asked for their help. Bless them. My children aren't even newborn but I do still need help and still live by my mantra; in fact

I'm now happy asking for the help I need. If there are people you can call on, do ask them; I do know how lucky I am to have help at hand. I also know, and they do, that I would gladly do the same for them should they ever need it. Having such a team around you can save you a fortune and really uplift you when chores or life seem too much.

Make sure people know how appreciated they are – you don't need to buy anything, a few words and a big hug is all it takes.

Recently a good friend paid for me to go to my slimming classes when I got a bit strapped for cash. Another took in my wet washing when my tumble-dryer broke, saving me from hours at the money-guzzling laundrette. I have just given the first friend my old baby-changing table and sorted out some great hand-me-down children's clothes for the second. It is okay to accept help – and there are always ways to return the favour.

CHAPTER 5

Your Newborn Baby (0–6 months)

A baby's needs are really very few, but sometimes we are faced with an overwhelming array of products that we can feel our babies really need. From feeding to nappies and what clothes and toys to invest in (as well as what not to buy), this chapter looks at your baby's basic needs from newborn to six months and offers creative ways to keep costs as low as possible.

32. MILK AND MONEY

As soon as your baby is born, milk is at the forefront of their minds – and yours. All healthcare professionals will advise you that breast is best, and you'll probably have covered breastfeeding in your antenatal classes or attended a workshop at the end of your pregnancy. Fact: breastfeeding is best for your baby and best for your pocket – it is completely free. Do stick with breastfeeding if you can; it is a skill and practice makes perfect. Visualise it and think positive. Prepare yourself: look at the pictures of positions, and ask friends who have done it for advice and to be on standby. If you like, you could watch an online video (just type 'breastfeeding video' into google). It is well worth the extra effort.

Of course, even in the recent past, we used to live in communities where the women who fed or had fed their babies shared their knowledge and skill, but now it is something we usually come across for the first time when we actually try to do it. I see breastfeeding a bit like riding a bike: it's hard as hell for some of us and it feels we will never get there, then once learned it seems as natural as walking. Some people get it straight away, some never get there. Don't struggle in silence, ask your health visitor or midwife or visit your local breastfeeding group and ask the mothers there. Keep on asking until you get the hang of it; if you prefer to talk to someone on the phone, call one of the many breastfeeding helplines (see page 247).

According to an online article from the BBC in July 2008 (www.bbc.co.uk/bloom/actions/breastfeed.shtml) formula feeding your baby for their first year can cost around £280. If you breastfeed you won't have to buy any formula milk; though you may have to invest in a steriliser and bottles, if you plan to express milk. Breastfeeding is convenient, portable and, what's more, is a wonderful bonding experience.

If, however, you can't get on with breastfeeding do not beat yourself up about it. I have known mums who were so intent on breastfeeding, keen and avid about the benefits, but it just didn't work out for them. Your baby needs a happy mum not a stressed-out, miserable one.

Feeding times when your baby's milk comes in a bottle can still be intimate and lovely experiences.

If you do use formula then buy powder rather than expensive cartons of ready-made milk. If you know you're going to be out of the house for a while, then take some measured-out formula powder in a container along with a bottle of cooled boiled water, then you have milk at the ready when you need it.

You'll find some useful phone numbers, websites and books about feeding support in the Resource Bank (page 247). I used a couple of these support services myself and they gave me great free advice.

A good relationship with your health visitor is invaluable and they can give you advice on formula feeding too. I changed my GP surgery to get the health visitor I wanted and I'm so glad – she was so supportive to me, throughout breastfeeding right through to my pre-school anxieties. If you aren't happy with your healthcare support do make changes. Health visitors are a lifeline.

33. NAPPIES THAT DON'T COST THE EARTH

You may well have been introduced to the vast array of nappy options during your antenatal classes. So, you'll know that nappies are a pretty immediate concern. Without them things could get pretty messy, pretty quickly. Disposable nappies are the most expensive option: a pack of 40 costs about £7. And since you will get through roughly a pack a week, that's about £30 a month on nappies. It soon mounts up.

In early 2007, the environment agency declared that there is little environmental difference between disposable and reusable or 'real' nappies, despite the popular belief that reusable are better. It took three years and £30million to decide the two had the same impact on the environment.

For many, however, reusable nappies are still considered greener and they are much cheaper than their disposable counterparts. According to most websites considering the 'great nappy debate', buying and washing your own nappies can save you up to £600 from birth to potty training for your first child. Now that's quite a saving – a holiday, at least.

Reusable nappies have come a long way since nappy pins and triangular terry towelling. Their popularity is often supported by local councils, who may hold events to promote real nappies and give away vouchers to subsidise a nappy service. Find out from your health visitor what schemes are available locally and do research online. Money-wise, various websites do better promotions than shops, but having a chat with a knowledgeable shop assistant is a fantastic introduction – you'll get a demonstration and a chance for a close look at all the nappy types.

In preparation for my son's birth I had bought a starter pack of newborn size real nappies. But because my son was premature and weighed only just over 3lb he didn't fit them. So, I started him off in disposables and, hate to say it, continued to use disposables from then on. I am ashamed to say I think we have used about 4,000 nappies since I made that initial decision. That's a lot of cash and a lot of landfill. Don't make the same mistakes as me, real nappies have worked well for lots of mums I know.

If you stick with disposables but want to do your bit for the environment then you could choose eco-disposables, which are recycled and/or biodegradable. These nappies are so popular that many supermarkets now stock them, though these types are more expensive than standard disposables. Supermarket own-brand nappies do a perfectly good job and can save you a significant amount of money.

Without exception everyone I know who began with real nappies and persisted past the first month continued through to potty training and on to child number two. Real nappies now come with the cutest covers and are super-easy to use.

34. DITCH THE NAPPY BAGS – EVERY LITTLE HELPS

Cheap as nappy bags are, there is nothing wrong with just folding a disposable nappy over really tight and popping it straight into the dustbin. Every little saving helps. Nursery catalogues and lists of what your baby needs might include a nappy wrapper bin, but these are an unnecessary luxury in my book. Just get those dirty nappies straight out of the house, is what I say.

35. BABY BATHS OR THE KITCHEN SINK?

Are baby baths a necessary expense? 'Why not just wash him in the sink?' my mum suggested to me, but I have to say I wasn't convinced. A little carrot peel stuck to your baby may be cute but an old tea bag? 'I meant the bathroom sink,' she said. Oh, well, that's different, I thought. But I found that wasn't too easy either in my sink with a tiny tot, let alone a slightly bigger baby; taps on their head, toes in the plughole, etc. Of course, if your kitchen has a lovely big sink, it may be perfect, for a while at least. Give it a try. I know someone who did actually use her kitchen sink (minus carrot peel I hasten to add) because it was the best height for her aching back.

All a baby really needs is for you to hold him for a couple of minutes and clean him in something that's big enough, safe, clean and holds water. I ended up holding both my babies in the same little baby bath, then in the shallows of the big bath (though that can be a killer on your back, depending on your bath) till they could sit up unsupported. I know many people who skipped a baby bath altogether and just put a little water in their big bath.

First time around, it's easy to buy every bath gadget going. You can have a floating bath support, a seat that looks like a potty to sit up in and a sort of stand with fabric for your baby to lie on. Why would a baby need three seats? There are cute little thermometers that tell you with a tick if the water is the right temperature, special top and tail bowls with fishes on and towels with special little hoods and ducks on that cost a fortune too, plus bath toy scoops shaped like frogs. All these are gimmicks. A cheap bath thermometer from a chemist, a Tupperware bowl and an ordinary towel, if soft and clean, work just as well. Until babies have been sitting up a while, you should always keep hold of them, and they are in and out of the bath so quickly they don't need lots of props. Later on, they'll want floating toys or plastic cups and bowls, which you can just borrow from the kitchen. Sharing a bath with your baby will absolutely delight him without the need for any toys – you are always the best free entertainment your baby could have.

Like many baby products, expensive baby baths are Western luxuries that are really unimportant – your baby couldn't care less. 'Mummy, why didn't I have a luxury bath with a duck thermometer and a floating light-up frog?' is not a question you will ever hear from your teenager. Don't waste your money on gimmicks – there are much better things to spend it on.

36. SHUN THOSE TOILETRIES TEMPTATIONS

All good books and health visitors will tell you that your baby should be bathed in nothing but plain water for the first few months and that their bottoms should be cleaned with just cotton wool and water. But this is not what the marketing people will tell you. They want you to buy one or more from the myriad products for babies on the market. It can be tempting to buy gorgeous-smelling toiletries for your baby with promises of lovely fragrances and soft skin, but these can be very expensive and are not at all necessary. Babies smell lovely as they are, so choose bath and skin products that are as simple as possible and perfume-free.

Nappy cream should be used sparingly and only when required. An oil, such as sunflower or grapeseed, can be used for moisturising baby's dry skin or for a massage after a bath; these oils are natural – and cheap.

Now there's a little one in the house, you may want to change your washing detergent. Wash baby clothes at low temperatures using a non-biological detergent – not only it is cheaper on your pocket, it is also better for the environment. You do not have to buy expensive brands, just make sure it's non-biological and fragrance-free. Line-dry your washing whenever you can, your washing will smell fantastic and you'll save a fortune on electricity by not using the tumble-dryer.

37. KITTING OUT YOUR BABY ON A BUDGET

Baby clothes can be expensive, which is a shame because apart from your baby they are the cutest things, and I am sure dressing your baby will bring you huge pleasure.

My baby girl was a 5lb bundle of skin and bone when she was born but this lasted for all of about five minutes as she went through a selection of:

- tiny baby clothes (5–7½lb)
- small baby clothes (7½–9¾lb)
- newborn baby clothes (up to 12lb)
- 0–3 months clothes (up to 14lb)

She set off on a superspeedy journey to over 14lb in just four months, but that meant that nothing from any of those clothing ranges fitted her any longer. She put on weight far faster than I would have anticipated. Most babies whizz through their wardrobe so there is no point building up a big selection in those early months.

Best investment clothes

There are some clothes, though, that last much longer than others and get more wear. Here are my top five investment pieces (I don't mean to sound like a fashion magazine).

1. Pinafores – These can be long then mini. As long as the armholes are roomy they can last quite a while.
2. Dungarees – Choose those with two-button straps to give you extra length so they'll fit as long as they go round their tummy.
3. Trousers with a turn-up or fold-up – The fold-up can be let down later. I also found jersey trousers (aka leggings) a good buy: these stretched comfortably to fit and if they were a size too big a little turn-up at the bottom looked just fine.
4. Pyjamas and bundlers – Any nightwear without built-in feet will last you longer. Bundlers (baby nighties with an elasticated bottom to keep your little one snug as a bug) and pyjamas last longer than sleepsuits as they usually have lots of room for movement. Little legs grow fast and sleepsuits will start to strain (unless, that is, you cut the feet off). If you prefer your baby to sleep in all-in-ones then choose plain white sleepsuits (which tend to be cheaper): they can be thrown into the wash with the muslins, and can be worn under other clothes to keep baby cosy. You can also wash them on hot for stubborn stains if you need to.
5. A sleeping bag – If you have a baby that likes to throw off blankets and then wakes up cold in the night, then a sleeping bag is ideal: it will keep baby snug and warm at night. These come in six-monthly size stages and they really do last the distance.

Best budget baby clothes

However much you like to dress up your baby, bear in mind that in the first few years your baby will not care one jot what they're wearing. If you don't care either, don't buy into it. Keep your baby snuggled, cuddled, clean and well fed and they will be happy. Dressing babies and kids in designer outfits and coordinated get-ups is a grown-up pastime. So, get shopping savvy and choose your baby's wardrobe wisely.

SUPERMARKET SWEEP – A quarter of all clothes in the UK are bought at supermarkets and popping an outfit in with the weekly shop has become a habit for many shoppers. Choose wisely and you can create several lovely outfits out of just a few key pieces, all of which won't cost much. If you don't want your baby to look like every other local baby then visit a different supermarket a little bit further away as they all tend to have slightly different stock. My little girl had a £2 Asda hat that looked French and gorgeous. It wasn't bought from a local Asda so nobody else I knew had one like it. I lost count of the number of compliments I got for that hat.

BARGAIN HUNT – Always head for the high street at sale time, but do go with an idea in mind of what you need. Next, Mothercare and babyGap have brilliant sales and you can stock up on what you need for the next sizes up.

SECOND TIME AROUND – Buying second-hand is down to the individual, as I've said before, but with a good wash and a press often that second-hand item turns out to be a gorgeous number that you could never have afforded new. I know a really enterprising woman who runs a business buying up designer baby clothes from mums then selling them onto other mums through craft fairs and on an appointment-only basis. She'll turn up with cases of designer baby clothes in the size you've requested and you sift through. It's brilliant and she does amazingly well.

BORROWED CLOTHES – As with borrowing baby equipment (see page 55), you may be able to borrow a large amount of the clothing you need for the first six months. But do be aware that, if your friend or relative wants things back, very young babies are sick easily, poo often escapes out of the nappy and stains from purees can be almost impossible to remove. So either borrow only as a last resort or be prepared to replace if necessary. If you're worried about staining items, just make sure you pop on a bib during feeding times, or do as my friend Sarah does (and she has the most immaculately dressed twins ever) and simply take their nice clothes off when they eat at home and have mealtimes in their nappies.

HAND-ME-DOWNS – Accepting hand-me-downs is a smart move; people rarely pass on rubbish and since babies tend to stain clothes pretty quickly (when they're weaning anyway) nothing stays pristine for long. I love dressing my children in nice clothes and, fortunately, I have the most wonderful friends who have consistently passed on items as soon as their kids have outgrown them. Do accept anything you are given, you can always pass on the goodwill to someone else if it's not to your taste. Do pass the clothes on again when you are done with them. This cycle of sharing saves everyone money and means the garment gets its true wear. Don't be proud. No one need ever know.

Make the most of the clothes you have by looking after them; any item that's clean, ironed and mended always look good. No money required, just time and effort.

Pester power

In the future, from as early as the age of two, your child may well start to ask for specific items that you're not keen on or that you wouldn't or couldn't buy. That Spiderman T-shirt or Dora trainers that flash may become your child's total focus and you should be prepared for regular pestering. On such occasions I have found exactly what my son has wanted and then asked Grandma or Aunty Jane to get it for Christmas, Easter or his birthday. If none of these occasions are close and he or she really can't live without it (and you can't live with the pestering) I have sometimes raided the piggy bank. Sometimes you child wants to be like all his or her friends, but you are the one in control of their wardrobe and the purse. Often you can offer a compromise if you can't bear that Fifi jumper or those Thomas the Tank pyjamas by explaining that you don't have the money for that but that you can find something cheaper – a Dora pencil case or a Thomas sticker book. Children can be totally understanding about money and they're not materialistic at all, so don't feed into their desires to be like the next kid at every turn. (When they're older, you can indulge them more on the fashion front – skinny jeans and Hannah Montana sparkles or Vans and baggy combats; just try to remember what it was like for you when you wanted pointy shoes or drainpipe jeans – first time around!).

I kept many of my son's baby clothes only to have a girl second time round. Although the time of year was the same, the weather was very different and even the neutral shorty all-in-ones weren't worn due to size differences. I only reused vests and sleepsuits in the end. Some clothes probably won't be right for baby number two unless, that is, you have babies of the same gender, same weight and who are born at the same time of year. If you're not passing them down, it's a good idea to sell on clothes soon after they've been outgrown as fashions change. Selling after each age stage will pay for the kitting out of the next.

For how to sell your items see Chapter 11 (page 204).

38. RESIST THE TOY TEMPTATIONS

For the first six months there won't be much your baby needs in the way of toys. His or her main entertainment is from you, along with a sprinkling of free and natural props. You really don't need to invest in huge amounts of plastic. At this age my baby girl liked to hold a straw, suck her blanket, look at her daddy and watch our cat. She liked to pull my hair, look in the bathroom mirror, watch her big brother and stare at her hands. She liked to have a swing on my knee, be massaged and cuddled, and have stories read to her. She liked to stare at trees and clouds, watch the ducks being fed and to see her little friends, too. Lisi loved her milk, being sung too, riding about in her pram, watching the washing machine, and, if I was desperate for some peace and quiet, watching CBeebies. Such free entertainment just requires time and thought. If I wanted to treat her, a 50p bottle of bubbles would absolutely delight her and last ages; in fact I now carry a bottle with me for instant entertainment.

I'm not saying don't buy any toys. Babies do need stimulation: in the car, in the pram or when you want a break and toys encourage their development. Most toys can be bought as birthday or Christmas presents; let relatives or friends know what you want beforehand.

Popular baby toys

A survey of my mummy friends gave me this list of toys that seem to be the most popular and cost effective in those first few months:

○ some little books with black-and-white pictures (easily borrowed form the library)

○ a mobile (get one on eBay, they get very little wear so second-hand mobiles tend to be in excellent condition)

○ a cuddly toy (cheap and cheerful works just fine)

○ a blankie (will someone knit you one?)

○ a few different rattles

○ an activity mat (borrowed or second-hand is best as these can be expensive)

○ a mirror (one of yours is fine but do supervise if using real glass; a cheap plastic one is even better)

○ a ball to roll (scrunched-up paper will do)

○ a teething ring (or anything clean that they can't choke on and is chewy)

○ a pretend remote control (or a clean one with no batteries – babies bizarrely and universally seem to love these, as well as mobile phones and keys!)

Search online for anything you really want for your baby to find it as cheaply as possible or scour your local car boot sale. Use that baby money you feel you should be saving, after all it's been given for the baby, right? The best toys I ever bought were those I had seen my children enjoying at other people's houses. Knowing they really liked something made buying it a smart decision – a twist on 'try before you buy'.

39. SOCIALISING NOT SHOPPING

Getting out and about with other mums and babies is vital; otherwise you may get really fed up cooing and gooing, feeding and nappy changing all day long, alone. It is also great for your baby too, to make some 'friends' along the way and learn to socialise. It is fairly easy to make baby mum friends. In Chapter 3 (see page 69) I suggested starting this at the antenatal stage; hopefully these friendships, with a little bit of effort, will have endured, even blossomed and will soon become your salvation.

If your antenatal classes didn't bear fruit on the mummy friend front, finding new ones is pretty straight forward. Head to the park on a sunny day, the health centre on baby weigh-in day, try out a baby class or attend a mother-and-baby group (see page 109). It's not the finding of other mums and dads that is usually the problem, it is initiating friendships that can feel a bit like that first day at school. Take a deep breath. Babies are a great conversation starter and a huge leveller. We have all run out of nappies and been vomited on when the baby wipes are missing. (Or is that just me?) Just speak up, smile and see where it goes. Be brave, suggest coffee at yours and playdates in the park. Other parents will, I promise, be keen to build up friendships too. You will have to do this only once or twice for something good to come out of it. It really is worth it. You will have a place to go to for a free cup of tea, someone to talk to, share things with and, very importantly, it will save you just going out shopping or to a playcentre.

40. OUT AND ABOUT FOR 50p

Mother-and-toddler groups (although they should really be called 'carer and toddler' groups so Grandma, Dad or childminders don't feel excluded) are, in my opinion, fantastic. In my area, there is a different one on each day of the week. For a small charge (from 50p to £1.50), you and your baby will usually get a drink and biscuit as well as a craft activity, a lovely sing-along, a story and loads of different toys to play with. They are a great place to go for very little cash and offer an ideal location for making new friends – for both of you. You'll hear from other parents there about what's going on locally and which other groups are good too.

Stepping through the door of a mother-and-toddler group can be a bit daunting initially, especially if you are on your own. But once your baby's out of the buggy, you'll probably be so busy you won't feel self-conscious for long and you'll soon get chatting. Why not ask a friend or two to go with you if you're feeling nervous about going on your own? And if you're a regular, keep an eye out for newcomers or another mum or dad who may be desperate for a friendly word.

Many of your friends from your antenatal classes may go back to work, so don't limit your social circle – you can never have enough friends with babies. And if you hear about a mother-and-toddler group, don't be put off – lots of people take small babies to these, especially if they've already got a toddler. I took my three-month-old little girl – she loved to look at other babies, lying on a mat and jiggling to the singing. At six months she was listening to the story and shaking a rattle. Try a few and find one that is right for you and your baby.

41. BABY ACTIVITY CLASSES – TRY BEFORE YOU BUY

Pretty much all babies in their first six months love to swim, to listen and move to music, be massaged, do some yoga (though they won't know it's yoga) and relax. These days, depending on where you live, there are classes offering all such things. Some people talk about 'hot housing' babies – rushing them to grow up by attending classes on some kind of timetable – but in my experience such classes offer opportunities for parents to meet other parents and for babies to have fun trying new activities and seeing other babies.

I have loved all the classes I have tried (and believe me I have tried a lot). I am going to give you the low-down on those I attended and leave you to find out what's on near you. In the Resource Bank (page 241) you'll find some great websites that will link you to various local classes. Offline, details of local classes are posted at Sure Start centres, on library noticeboards, noticeboards at the health centre or GP surgery, small ads in family magazines and in local papers. Local churches are also a good source of information (as classes are often run in church halls). The best source of free information is word of mouth, so get chatting to other parents.

Activity classes can seem costly but I'm going to give you some tips to help you afford them and some advice on how you might replicate them at home. Below, I outline the classes I'm familiar with so you have an idea of the sorts of things on offer.

Baby signing

This was my favourite baby class (I liked it so much, I bought a franchise and taught it for two years!). At these classes you teach your baby to sign with their hands before they can talk. At five months' old my little girl could say she was thirsty without having to cry – she just made the milk sign with her hands. Fantastic! That saved us both loads of frustration.

The classes are relaxed and enjoyable. You learn the signs through singing nursery rhymes and action songs. At Tinytalk, the baby signing company I worked for and whose classes I attended with both my children, you sign and sing for half an hour. Then, you have a cup of coffee and some yummy biscuits while your baby plays with fabulous toys and you get to chat with other mums or dads for the next half hour. Both my children adored these classes. Their ability to communicate with me, long before their speech kicked in, has been both enlightening and amazing. My son, age four, signed to his baby sister to ask her if she wanted a drink or food. Classes are aimed at babies from birth till two years, but most people tend to start when their little ones are around four to six months. Babies tend to start signing from six to nine months. The various companies offering classes tend to have expansive websites with research articles, so do check them out (see also page 244). I promise you baby signing is fun as well as being a useful activity to do with your baby.

Alternatively, you can teach your baby to sign at home. This is a much cheaper option but is less sociable. To teach your baby to sign you just need to understand their development process, know a few signs and how to use them. You do have to be enthusiastic and dedicated too but, hey, that's free. See the Resource Bank (page 244) for class details.

Aquababies

Many swimming pools run baby-only swimming classes where you don't have splashy toddlers or overexcited 10-year-olds nearly jumping on your tiny baby's head. Most are based around songs with actions, and each week the class takes a similar form; this repetition helps your baby learn and makes them familiar with what's to come. At the classes I took my son to we used to sing 'Twinkle Twinkle Little Star' as we floated our babies on their backs, and 'Humpty Dumpty' as we helped them jump off the side into the water. It was a serene and gorgeous half hour.

I attended these classes for nearly two years. As our babies got bigger many of the mums in the class would take a packed lunch for them to eat in the nearby park after their swim – a lovely, sociable time. I have just started again with my baby daughter. Daddy sometimes goes instead of me as he gets lots of fuss from the impressed mums but he didn't have to be too sociable as it was a class. Dads (and I am generalising here) tend to prefer classes to toddler groups as there is a focus and they don't have to infiltrate mummy chats.

Almost every baby swimming class is a term commitment. If you don't want to book a course and make a regular and often expensive commitment, check out the parent and baby sessions at your local leisure centre. During these sessions in the week the pool is lovely and calm, often the inflatables or floats are out for all to use and you pay as you go.

Get hands on – baby massage

I was very lucky with my son – I had four free sessions of baby massage from my local health centre when he was about 10 weeks' old. These were great, not just because I got to meet other parents, but also because baby massage is fantastic. Tracey Winston, an IAIM practitioner in baby massage who I met through baby signing was finishing up her training in baby massage when I had my daughter, so I got to be her model (for free, hurray!). Her class was relaxed, lovely and informative. Annalise loved meeting the other babies, and having dedicated attention, as well as being stroked and tickled and cuddled. It was easy for me to learn to do it regularly at home. Regular massage can bestow immense benefits on babies; here Tracey Winston describes them:

Baby massage has been practised for many centuries in countries around the world. It provides quality one-on-one time for you and your baby to get to know each other better. This special time is a wonderful opportunity for you to learn about and respond to your baby's body language; which in turn makes your baby feel safe, secure, respected and loved.

Since baby massage includes all the elements of attachment, such as touch, eye contact, voice and smell, it may help to strengthen the relationship between parent and baby. Additional benefits are thought to include relief from colic, constipation, teething pains and excess mucus. Baby massage may also stimulate the circulatory, digestive and lymphatic system, while also aiding relaxation and improving sleep patterns. This is by no means an exhaustive list – there is not the space here to detail all the possible benefits.

To find a baby massage instructor in your area visit www.iaim.org.uk. The International Association of Infant Massage was founded by and is based on the work of Vimala McClure. Further information on baby massage may be found in her publication Infant Massage – A handbook for loving parents *(see page 242).*

I cannot recommend highly enough the beautiful bonding experience that massage gave me and my children. Once you have learned how to do it (whether from a book, DVD or a course) you can continue for years at home. The only ongoing cost is the oil.

Baby yoga

Again, this was taught at my local health centre for free for new mums. It was lots of fun stretching and moving to songs and great for baby's (and mum's) flexibility. Baby yoga can be taught from any time after a baby's six-week health check, but most practitioners do like to wait until babies are three months' old at least. Classes are on the rise and links to them can be found in the Resource Bank (see page 244). Many mums take what they learn from the free lessons and carry on with baby yoga at home. At such classes take a notebook and jot down any instructions you feel you may forget. Suddenly a class becomes much more cost-effective if you can replicate it later at home for free.

Baby relaxation classes

I have only been to one of these classes but it was brilliant. The babies all did a little yoga and had a little massage and then the lights were lowered, the music put on and the sensory experiences began. There were feather boas and bubbles, light tubes and fibre-optics, treasure boxes to explore and lovely snuggle rugs to wrap up in. My baby adored it and so did I – I nearly fell asleep. It was

Affordable ways to pay

Try before you buy – My golden rule for any activity class is to try before you buy. Most places will let you have one session free or a taster session, rather than asking you to book up an entire course. Some classes work on a drop-in basis, which is great since babies get sick, need injections and sleep at the most inconvenient times. I have never yet managed to attend any full course of baby classes.

Ask for a discount – If you are on a tight budget but are keen to try an activity, tell the group leader. Some will have a flexible approach and may be able to support your attendance. For example, if you help set up, make coffee or take the money at the door you may get a free session once a month. It's worth asking. If you are on benefits you may be eligible for a concessionary price, so don't be embarrassed to ask, it could save you money.

Get them as presents – Also (and this was how I afforded many of them), you can always ask for classes as a gift for your baby at birthdays or Christmas. Most people are happy to contribute towards these. My son's godparents regularly bought him swimming classes as a present – which was fantastic for him and for us, financially. We truly appreciated it every single week. Later on my children moved on to gymnastics and music classes, tennis and football lessons and I even flirted with the idea of Spanish. We have had lots of fun and it doesn't have to cost a packet.

cocooning; for an hour the world was totally about relaxing my baby with no distractions. The only reason I didn't go to another class was the price, but I found it easy to copy the ideas at home at no cost. I just needed to turn off the phone, put on our lava lamp and some music, get a soft blankie, get some tactile toys together and play with my little one. Closing off the world for an hour is a very good thing and both you and your baby will benefit from that special time.

CHAPTER 6

Time to Think About You (0–6 months post-baby)

I t's probably been a while since you thought about little else than your little bundle of a baby but now is time to pay attention to you. You are important too – you are a mother but you're also a partner, a friend and your own person. So, take care of yourself; I'll show you how to without breaking the bank.

42. STILL EATING FOR TWO?

By asking that question I am not in any way advocating a crash diet; after all crash dieting is dangerously unhealthy and no good for you or your baby. What I'm prompting you to think about is are you still eating those extras that may have sustained your pregnancy? Not only will munching on chocolate, crisps, croissants and pastries make you feel sluggish, they cost too much and will keep you firmly in your maternity clothes. By the time your baby is six months old, if you're still in some maternity clothes you are sure to be sick to death of them. So, work on getting back in to your old clothes – it'll save buying a whole new wardrobe in a bigger size and will help you feel good about yourself (which then stops you buying chocolate, buying bigger clothes, etc. It's a virtuous circle!).

If you decide that you want to follow a weight-loss programme post birth, please talk to your doctor or health visitor and wait at least a few months. Losing weight too fast can wreak havoc on your body and you still need a chance to recover.

That said, eating a good balanced diet and enough food is vitally important for revitalising energy levels, particularly if you are breastfeeding, and for helping to combat any sleep deprivation. Drink plenty of fluids, as being dehydrated can make you feel lethargic and listless, and with a small baby to look after you need all the energy you can muster. If you don't feel quite right, make an appointment to see your health visitor or doctor for some advice or a check up. At various times I have been both iron- and calcium-deficient and had to take supplements for a while. Babies are lovely but they can wear you out and with so much looking after to do you can forget to eat properly. Do eat regularly even if you are exhausted as it helps to keep you calm, energised and happy...which is good for your baby and good for you. By the way, if you breastfeed you burn off an extra 500 calories a day so make sure you are eating enough.

Tempting as it might be, don't go down the ready-meals route if you can help it – you need simple, fresh food rather than overprocessed, refined food. Have the odd moussaka or pizza in the freezer for those nights when neither of you can be bothered to cook, but try to make this the exception rather than the rule.

43. ECONOMICAL EXERCISE

Exercise is important not only for getting you back into your normal size clothes but also for feeling strong, awake and upbeat. Your body may never be quite the same after childbirth and breastfeeding but you are probably aiming for a body that's toned and trim, healthy and fit.

Don't start exercising straight after giving birth. We are all individuals and have different birth experiences and bodies. Talk to your doctor or health visitor before you begin exercising and find out how much/what you should do at first.

Claire Mockridge owns Mummies and Buggies a successful, specialist ante- and postnatal exercise company. She is a qualified ante/postnatal fitness instructor and member of The Guild of Pregnancy and Postnatal Instructors. With regard to new mothers and exercise, she states:

It is vitally important for new mums not to return to exercise too soon after having had their baby. As a guide, women should wait six weeks after a natural birth and 10 weeks following a C-section. New mums should also attend an exercise class run by a trained postnatal instructor to ensure that the exercises they are performing are safe and effective. Attending a mainstream aerobics or body conditioning class could potentially injure your joints, do irreversible damage to your abdominals/pelvic floor and generally be very uncomfortable on the breasts.

Power pramming

Claire runs specialist classes for mummies and their babies to exercise together, buggy-jogging around the park alongside other workouts. Such classes are a great idea to help new mums get fit safely, avoids the use of a babysitter and helps local mums to meet up. There are ever-more of these specialist classes. For details please see the Resource Bank (page 256).

It is easy to imagine you will run around a lot keeping up with a toddler, but with a baby it's just not going to happen unless you make it…they don't move that much. Classes are a good way to go. You could ask for them as a Christmas gift or a use a bit of baby money – after all a happy mum makes a happy baby. If you simply can't afford classes or are highly self-motivated, a regular morning jog or power walk around the park with your buggy is just the ticket. Exercise, like sex and chocolate, releases endorphins and these chemicals can help stave off the baby blues and help calm rampaging hormones, so make sure you get your free fix.

To gym or not to gym?

If you're a gym addict, then later on when your body is more back to normal you may want to think about rejoining the gym. But with crèche costs to find too, the gym is one luxury that may need to fall by the way side, for now at least.

Enjoy the freedom

Jogging, cycling, power walking, pram racing and roller blading are all pretty much free activities once you have the basic equipment. Regular exercise makes you look and feel fantastic, so investigate how you can build some in to your normal week. If you can get someone to give you a break just three times a week for about 20–40 minutes you could be fit and glowing in no time, and it won't have cost you a penny. Good times to nip out for a fast walk or run could be early evening when dad comes home from work, just let him have a coffee or a sit down first. You could be more flexible though and just take the opportunity to go for it when your neighbour/mum/friend pops over for a baby cuddle. Don't do this every time they pop over though or they may well get a bit fed up!

Workout with Davina

Another option is to pick up an exercise DVD for about 50p from a car boot or borrow one from the library and do it while your baby is in bed – that way you don't even need a sitter. You can be your own personal trainer if you're keen enough.

Motivational partners

Exercising with a friend is fun too and can keep you motivated. Could you pal up with another mum? My good friend Helen goes power walking with her mum friends now their toddlers are at preschool and they find it maintains their friendships and their figures for free.

44. ADVICE IS FREE

Advice from others costs nothing and so it has to be a good thing, right? Well, it may well save you money on books or consultations but I can tell you now advice comes from everyone – window cleaners, bus drivers, in-laws, governments, sisters, friends, work colleagues and your neighbours – when you have just had a baby. They all have an opinion on how you could be a better parent.

As a rule of thumb, the best advice (see, even I am at it now) is to ignore everyone, except perhaps for your health visitor and if she isn't on your wavelength then find one who is pronto (they are usually great, though). My health visitor was vigilant about my son's health and very, very kind, which is what I wanted most in the world and I felt I could tell her anything. She was better than any parenting book I could have bought.

Seek out people you trust and ask opinions if you want them. Other parents can be a gold mine of good ideas and suggestions. Their tips tend to be current, based on modern thinking and usually tried and tested – ask enough mums and one suggestion will normally work for you.

Following your health visitor's recommendations will keep you and baby as safe as possible so ask questions if you are unsure. Health visitors are guided by the

Department of Health and the World Health Organization – so they should be up to date. If Great Aunt Sally tells you to lay that crying baby of yours on its front, give it honey or smack its bottom to keep it quiet, you can just smile sweetly and say, 'We have been told by the doctor and our health visitor to follow the World Health Organization and Department of Health guidelines to keep them on their back at night, not give honey and not batter them.' You can then leave the room sharpish on the pretext of doing something, taking your crying baby with you. They will, no doubt, be gobsmacked by your serenity and all the professionals you have mentioned in one sentence – that should shut them up for a bit! Meanwhile, you can take a big breath and plan your escape route.

45. BABYSITTING FOR BISCUITS

When you feel that you've finally got a handle on day-to-day life, you'll be ready for a night out. Now, though, on top of the cost of going out, you'll have the extra expense of a babysitter, unless you give these cash-friendly options a try. The most important factor about any babysitter is that it is someone who you trust completely. You wouldn't leave your car keys with a random stranger, so don't leave your baby unless you're totally happy with the person who's sitting.

Friends and family

In the early days, a social life with a baby can seem to be an impossibility, but it is really important to try to keep a life for you and your partner. In my opinion the best babysitters are the ones who do it for free and out of love, perhaps Grandma or your best friend. Make sure it is someone you know inside out. The golden rules of gratis babysits are: don't ask too often, don't be late, be sure they get home safe (if it's at night), make sure the kids are in bed (if it's at night), leave everything they need out and easy to find, and be contactable at all times. Yummy biscuits help, too.

Babysitting swaps or circles

Many groups of mums get together and set up a babysitting circle. Such systems can be as simple or complicated as you like, involving turns or tokens rather than any money. There are free guides to how to set up babysitting circles online, so do some research if that's what you prefer. Another, more flexible idea, is to swap with just one or perhaps two other mum friends. By keeping the numbers small, you gain on flexibility and last-minute invitations and your children will always know the person sitting, in case they wake up or need something while you're out.

Payment in kind

If Grandma sits often, maybe you could weed her garden while she looks after your baby one day? Everyone's a winner – you get a breather and some exercise, your baby gets lots of cuddles from Grandma and Grandma's garden is tidy. What could be better?

46. TREAT YOUR PARTNER (WITH LOVE)

It's easy for men to feel pushed out of the very intimate mummy–baby bond in the first few months of family life. They are used to having you all to themselves so having someone else, however small, stealing their loved one can be tough. With money possibly being tighter, it's not quite so easy for him to buy you flowers or for you to stock up on his favourite beer as often as you'd both like. But, you can still show your love for each other without the need for money. Here are some ideas for relationship lifters that cost only time and effort.

Massages and more

Just a little massage, whether it is neck and shoulders or a full back and legs can make your partner feel wonderful and re-energised. If you're lucky, he might return the favour. Set the scene with a few candles dotted around the room to create the mood for a bit of a cuddle afterwards.

A luxurious soak

Be spontaneous: greet your partner on his return home with a bath with your best bubbles, low lighting and a glass of wine or a cold beer and perhaps some music turned on low. Go on, spoil him. It'll take you all of 10 minutes to prepare but will feel like real luxury to the receiver.

As easy as ABC

Once your baby is down for the night, a romantic meal for two can sound like a massive effort. But what makes a meal special is not the effort poured into making something complicated and expensive. It is as simple as ABC.

A – Actually going out and getting your partner's favourite food.

B – Beautiful presentation – perhaps a flower in a vase, the best plates and cutlery and a little candle.

C – Clearly having made an effort – clothes without dribble on would be a good start, maybe a dot of perfume and a big, bright smile, even if you're tired. These take mere minutes and a little effort goes a long way.

Scrabble anyone?

It's all too easy to slump on the sofa and zone out in front of the TV when you have both had a tiring day, which is fine from time to time, but not every night. Instead, do something different – dig out that old Scrabble board, dust off the chess set or plan your dream holiday, you'll be rewarded by some close and relaxing time with your partner.

The power of touch

Cuddles and holding hands don't require you to feel sexy, shave your legs and put on great underwear, but they are gentle, important reminders to the one you love that you still adore him. Don't forget that small things can mean the world. You cuddle your baby every day, don't you, so make sure the other love of your life – your partner – doesn't miss out either.

Love notes

A little love note slipped into a lunch box or a briefcase, left on a desk or in the fridge can be a sweet reminder that you really do care. Everyone benefits from being told they're loved, and this may be needed more than ever if you have been particularly tired or irritable lately. Days can feel lonely for our partners when we are devoted to our new babies. Take those few seconds to write a love note – the thought will affect the receiver all day. Loving texts are great too but nothing tops a handwritten note.

Say thank you

Appreciate the support and love you receive and make a habit of always saying 'thank you' and spelling out what for. It is easy to become so wrapped up in being a parent and our baby's needs that we forget to look outwards and others can end up feeling taken for granted. Saying thank you can make all the difference.

Time off for dads, too

Every parent needs time off, just to be by themselves. You'll probably be more vocal about having some baby-free time and your space as a mummy than your partner, but do make sure they have some 'me time' too. In my house on a Saturday morning I get a lie-in, breakfast in bed and often the whole morning to do just as I want. On a Sunday morning my other half gets exactly the same. It works for us. Find something that works for you and gives you both some time off. This precious 'me time' will keep you both sane.

47. NIGHTS OUT ON THE CHEAP

Keeping yourself in circulation with old (non-baby) friends is crucial to remembering who you are and enjoying life to the full. You may feel constrained by a small budget but going out needn't cost much. Here are a few creative ideas for a purse-friendly social life.

Nights out with the girls

Meals out with your girlfriends are a great chance to catch up and are a real treat: a delicious, relaxing meal and you don't have to wash up afterwards. Time your evenings out after your baby goes down at night, so there's no need to rush. Try to arrange to be near enough so that you can pop home if need be. Scout around for quality and value restaurants (see page 272 for any vouchers doing the rounds) and don't discount BYO restaurants, they often work out cheaper.

Join the club

Book clubs are a brilliant way of spending no cash (order books through the library), using your brain and having a cheap evening without any baby talk. It is easy to set up a book club – just contact a bunch of your friends who you know like to read, choose a book and arrange for them to come to your house one evening. Wine and nibbles are optional, but tea won't impact on your early starts and costs far less. Plenty of guidelines on how to run a book club can be found online, but basically you chat about what you thought of the book, choose your next book and have a good old natter. With a fairly new baby, you spend quite a lot of time sitting down feeding. Join a book club and you'll always have something to hand to read. Most importantly it is a pre-arranged social event that keeps you in contact with friends and keeps you sane. It's usual take it in turns to host the club but if you are the only one with a little baby and you want to stay close to home, speak up – just take it in turns to bring the biccies.

Remember the good ol' days?

Have your best friend over for an evening after your baby has gone to bed, have a giggle over old photos and old boyfriends, play your old Bon Jovi/Bananarama/Duran Duran CDs (or is that just me?) and remember fond times from your life before having a baby. Share a homemade pizza and have some fun. It'll be a real treat.

Clothes swap

Get the girls over for a clothes swap or organise a Swap It party (see page 169). Ask everyone to bring one or two items of clothes they are willing to part with, along with a bottle of wine. Trying on is bound to produce plenty of laughter, plus you can come away with new clothes. Perfect.

Retail therapy

A girl has to go shopping once in a while, whether for food, for birthday gifts or just for some new knickers. Take a shopping list and only as much money as you can afford and then head off with a friend for an hour or two. Little babes often enjoy a bus ride or a push around town and you don't have to splash out on lunch – grab a bench and eat your sandwiches together. Fit in free friend time wherever you can.

Many of the things you did with your friends before you had a baby can still be enjoyed. You just need to adjust your expectations slightly.

CHAPTER 7

Weaning, Walking and Wearing You Out (6–24 months)

From six months old your baby will start to move, eat and chatter. Babies start to get cross if they don't get what they want and generally become much more interactive and interesting, but a lot more demanding, too. In this chapter we'll look at the up-and-coming areas in your baby's life and how to fund any absolutely essential purchases along the way.

48. FOOD FOR THOUGHT

Once your baby is ready for weaning (at about six months), suddenly costs can spiral – you need bibs, a highchair, bowls, plates, lots of freezer containers and the food itself. I would strongly recommend making these first foods yourself, as lots will be wasted: mouths missed, spit up in your hair, down their clothes, etc. Jars of baby food can be expensive, whereas a few pounds of apples, sweet potatoes, carrots or squash cost little by comparison and make lots of baby meals. Don't feel your days are going to be spent, apron-clothed in your kitchen cooking, puréeing and freezing in batches. It's easy enough to fit most cooking alongside your evening meals. For example, if you are having broccoli with your sausage and mash just cook a little extra broccoli, purée it and then pop it in the freezer for your baby for another day. A handy way is to freeze such food in ice-cube trays, then pop them out and keep the cubes in freezer bags; then take whatever you need from the bag, defrost and heat up as required.

When my son was a baby, my mum would make us a lovely macaroni cheese and cauliflower cheese once every few weeks. I would purée and freeze some of these as little meals for him. If your baby is lucky to have family nearby, then food infused with 'Grandma love' can save you the time and energy required to prepare healthy and nutritious food for you and your baby. So, if there's a budding MasterChef in the family or your circle of friends, let them know what your favourite foods are and see what they come up with.

Having a good cookbook of baby and toddler meals on the shelf means you need never run out of ideas. Healthy food does not have to be expensive, just well considered and cooked with fresh ingredients. I've included many of my favourite cookbooks in my book list at the back of the book (see page 251). Like me, my children are both vegetarian, and my health visitor was fantastic at supporting me in terms of ensuring their diet was balanced and complete.

Food on the run

It is a good idea to take your own snacks when you go out. Babies need to eat little and often; energy slumps result in grumpy babies. Breadsticks, rice cakes, raisins, squares of cheese and chopped fruit all make great cost-saving snacks (keep them in an air-tight container or resealable bag) that are ready in a moment if you are out and about or bump into a friend and stop for a quick coffee. Packaged juice drinks or designer bottles of water are a waste of money when home-prepared drinks taste exactly the same. If your baby likes to drink out of squidgy bottles get a funky one and keep filling it up. If you're smart and prepared, then you'll reap the rewards.

Mini lunches

If an outing coincides with a mealtime consider taking your baby's lunch with you, as many 'child's meals' never get eaten. Some cafés and restaurants will even heat up food pots if you ask them. Or opt for the cold-plate option of lots of bits like cheese, fruit, crackers, etc. Alternatively, share your lunch with your little one, just ask for an extra side plate and serve them a mini lunch that way.

49. A NO-NONSENSE NURSERY

The Department of Health recommends (at the time of writing) that a baby sleeps in a parent's room until they are at least six months old. Moving your baby into his or her own room is a major life event that can suddenly feel like a very expensive one. Depending on your home, you may have to consider decorating, buying a cot and putting up blackout blinds. It's all too easy to spend a lot of money on nursery bits-and-bobs – co-ordinating furniture, bedlinen that matches nappy stackers, curtains that go with rugs, even light-switch covers that continue the theme. You can avoid such nursery nonsense and stick to the basics.

My best friend bought me a second-hand cot and a new mattress. It has been perfect for both my babies and I will pass it on when the time is right. In our baby son's room, we painted the walls white and used easy-to-apply (and easy to peel off!) stickers to brighten the walls. We borrowed a lava lamp (one of those glass tubes that stands upright with changing lights and bubbles that float up and down) from a friend who ignored it in his home office. It mesmerised our babies and relaxed us too. Our good friend who sells blinds (very handy) put up blackout blinds for free when we were broke and sleep deprived. What a star! We assembled a flat-pack chest of drawers and relocated an old CD player. That was it – a simple, stylish nursery at a snip.

Large nursery items can be pricey so shop around, consider second-hand and as always ask for what you want at birthdays and Christmas. Remind yourself that your baby really will not care if the duvet cover does not match the light shade. Cosy and warm, calming and safe are all that are required of a nursery.

50. SHOES ON A SHOESTRING

Babies often start to crawl then walk from anything from seven to 16 months. Once they're upright and cruising around, shoes become an expensive part of life. Expensive because babies feet grow so quickly, then later because they get scuffed and worn through and because often you need more than one pair. Shoes get soaked in puddles and filled with sand so don't get too attached to that nostalgic image of lovely baby shoes – they don't stay that way for long. Don't think that toddlers need as many pairs of shoes as you; really all they need are one pair of shoes (canvas ones in summer) and a pair of wellies – anything else is extra. When the price of your baby's shoes comes close to a pair for you, you'll soon make sure you look after their shoes (keep an eye out for those that get pulled off and thrown from the buggy!).

My philosophy is this: in the house socks are fine, as are bare feet – let their feet breathe. As long as no one else wears shoes and the floors are clean there is no need for slippers, unless your house is freezing. Supermarket wellies are cheap and perfectly adequate. (Cute wellies shaped like crocodiles will only keep your child amused for so long and it's literally the difference between £2 and £20.) In winter, trainers have a good grip and are durable. Plus they wash easily (always a bonus).

Shoes are a wholly suitable gift to ask for at Christmas or birthdays and one grandparents often love to buy, particularly if you let them take their darling grandchild to have them fitted. To avoid any expensive disasters, though, point out the ones you approve of first.

51. PARKS, PUDDLES AND PICNICS

Local parks are an absolute lifeline for all parents – they cost nothing and open all year round.

Parks tend to be free of big kids on a weekday (till 3.30pm when schools empty out), well maintained by the council, safe, help your little one expend loads of energy and they usually have a bench for you to rest your weary legs. Plus, they offer countless ways of having fun for free. Don't let the rain put you off. Grab everyone's wellies and waterproofs and brave the weather no matter what. Once children have run off their excess energy and got some fresh air they'll be much better behaved; what's more, all that fresh air and puddle jumping will perk you up no end. It's also a good place for making new friends, picking up leaves for pictures, having races and getting to grips with pedalling a trike. Kids of all ages adore picnics, there's something we all love about eating in the fresh air. Plus you don't have to sweep up all the usual crumbs. Even if your baby isn't walking, a little swing and a play in the sandpit is great stimulation.

If your park isn't up to scratch get campaigning to your local councillor or MP or, indeed, anyone who will listen. You can comment on your local park at www. greenstat.org.uk. Greenstat gives people the opportunity to say what they think about the quality of their open spaces and how well they feel they are being managed and maintained. This written information is then passed to the managing organisation of the park, most usually the local council. Many councils have signed up to the scheme; check if yours has and if it hasn't perhaps you should suggest it does. A list of affiliated councils is on the website. Writing and complaining to a local newspaper can often help too. Do take action if you need to – your local park is going to be a vital part of your life for many years to come.

52. LOVING YOUR LIBRARY

Now you've become reacquainted with your library, you'll discover that it's a hive of activity and often they have baby and toddler-centred sessions – singalongs and story times,which are fun and, more importantly, free. They are a great place to meet other mums, dads, grannies and babies. While you're there, you can also borrow CDs, videos and DVDs as well as storybooks for your baby. I can take out about 16 books at one time at my local library (though that makes for a heavy bag to carry home!). Head inside on a rainy day and you can colour in, read books and go on the computer safe in the knowledge that no one is going to kick you out. Borrowing library books is a bit like 'try before you buy'. If my son really takes to a particular book and wants it again and again and again, then that is enough for me to buy it for him. Books aren't cheap but if you know they're going to be loved, then they're priceless.

Obviously, information books (think weaning, recipes, toddler tantrums and play ideas) are available for you to borrow as well as the latest fiction titles. Borrowing is still blissfully free; but do be aware that although children's books don't incur fines for being overdue, your books do. To avoid excessive fines, keep all your library books in their own bag or box and put them back after reading, you'll be so pleased you have.

53. TV – TANTALISINGLY FREE

If you don't count the licence fee, TV is free and, used wisely, can be a great resource. I am one of the meanest TV mummies I know, even though I am with my kids almost all the time. I think this is largely due to my own dependence on it to relax, which I am continually trying to break. As with eating habits, I want my kids to do as I say not as I do, and so I ration TV to about half an hour a day.

However, TV costs nothing and it can be a useful distracter. I have also found 'TV time' buys me valuable minutes for an essential chore. The BBC channel for under-sixes, CBeebies, is great since it doesn't have advertising and almost everything is both educational and entertaining. Use TV wisely, just don't let it take over.

My advice is to use the TV to spark ideas for things you and your child can do together. For instance, I used to watch *Doodle Do* (an arts and crafts show) with my little boy, then we'd have a go ourselves at doing the activity. And after watching *Big Cook Little Cook* we'd try the recipe. Animals seen on *Our Planet* would inspire us to draw pictures or talk about animal sounds. If you use TV as a springboard as well as a 'temporary babysitter' – it can be an extremely useful resource.

54. PLAYDATES THAT DON'T COST A PENNY

Playdates are a chance for babies and parents to get together and play. Whether in a park, at a playcentre, at a swimming pool or at someone's house – these are great opportunities for you both to socialise. Playdates can cost nothing (a play at the park) or can cost the earth (a theme park).

If you can't afford a playdate you are invited to, just make up an excuse. But if you are comfortable do say, 'That's a bit expensive for us, how about we meet at the park or you come to ours another day.' That way the other parent knows you are keen to meet up and you're not just turning them down. If they don't follow through and take you up on your offer of a cheaper playdate or if they appear to look down on you because you don't have much money, then ditch them. You want friends who value you and your kids for who you are, not what you can afford.

It's tempting when hosting a playdate to rush out and buy lots of drinks, cakes or biscuits and madly straighten your house, get new pens, paper, etc. Resist the urge and relax. You don't want other parents made to feel inadequate by your 'perfect' house; everyone with kids knows what houses really look like during the day. Put on a big smile, put away your child's favourite toys (always a smart move) and get out the snacks and drinks your child would normally have. A warm welcome and a bit of patience is all that is needed to be a good host

P.S. Allocate one to two hours for a playdate – in my experience it falls apart soon after that.

55. NEW TOYS FOR NOTHING

Children do get bored seeing the same toys day in day out, so why not consider recycling them? I don't mean giving them to the charity shop; instead circulate your child's playthings – put some away in a cupboard for a while and bring them out again at a later date. Your baby will think they are new and rediscover them afresh. A toddler will play with an old baby toy in a completely different way six months down the line. Don't just get rid of something because the age it is specified for has passed. My seven-month-old baby loved my son's big dumper trucks and would happily sit spinning wheels. Conversely, he loved launching himself at her jungle-themed playmat (aged three) pretending he was an explorer.

If you don't have that many toys or books, why not swap with a good friend or two? I say good friends because rips, breaks and drool need to be forgiven and almost expected. I have successfully borrowed and lent children's books, toys and DVDs. If you don't get something you've lent back just don't lend to that person again. Generally, though, people are pretty good at returning things; sometimes a prompt along the lines of your toddler has been missing it and could you have it back please will work.

Another world of toys for discovery is a toy library. Not all areas have them, it depends on where you live, but some even have mobile versions. Check out the Resource Bank (page 257) to find out if you have one near you. Playgroups, toddler groups and little friends' houses all offer plenty of opportunities for playing with different toys.

As well as those toys you buy in the shops, free toys are all around us, just waiting to be discovered. Nature provides its own toys in the form of pine cones, conkers and piles of leaves, shells, soil and trees. Your home will provide its own toy possibilities, too; under the bed becomes a cave, blankets over a clothes horse become a den, sofas make great puppet theatres and chairs make a bus. You don't need to provide too many toys, otherwise all these free resources will remain untapped. Being a bit bored is sometimes crucial to stimulating a child's imagination and finding the fun in the world around them.

My top 10 toys for under-threes

Toys are exciting to children and they truly need a selection of things to keep them amused and stimulate their development.

Things to build with – Whether stacking cups, Duplo or Mega Blocks, all children love to build. And if you don't have a tub of bricks or cups, then just use cushions or even small books – all that's needed is a stackable tower that can be knocked down and rebuilt, over and over again.

Cuddly toys – Every child loves a cuddly, whether it be a bunny, a blankie or a soft dolly, most children have at least one favourite thing to cuddle. If your toddler becomes really attached to something, seriously consider buying another in case the first one gets lost or broken. My son's bedtime friend is a scrappy tiger we won at a fair; now I never let tiger leave the house (except once for a family photo!) as to lose him would be disastrous.

A paddling pool – Cheap to buy and giving hours of fun, a paddling pool is not just for the summer. Choose a smallish one (otherwise it'll take ages to fill and be too deep) that's brightly coloured. Come winter-time, bring it inside and fill it with multicoloured balls for your baby to 'splash' about in.

Musical instruments – Whether it's banging a drum (think saucepan and wooden spoon) or shaking home-made maracas (plastic bottles filled with rice or pasta), children of all ages love to make noise, but you can call it music. Get them to play along to a favourite CD while you're making the lunch.

Ride-on toys – All kids love to clamber aboard vehicles or animals that move along and negotiate the house on wheels. Be they trains, cars, trikes, baby walkers, scooters or donkeys, your baby is bound to have fun. I've found that car boot sales are great places to pick up second-hand ride-ons, as they can be pricey new. Of course, you don't need to buy anything: a supermarket shopping box slides really well across a laminate floor, as does a cardboard box. If you do buy a ride-on, look after it and don't let it rot in the garden. We have a £2 ride-on motorbike that has had far, far more use than the £50 car bought brand new.

Copying toys – By which I mean their own little tea set, tool kit, baking set or sweeping brush, anything that enables them to imitate what grown-ups do. Don't be fooled into thinking you need cough up for a pretend kitchen; when you cook, just give them a plastic bowl with some rice or dried beans and a wooden spoon. Kids love to help so get them on board as young as possible; my kids were soon helping for real, even if it was just putting a sock in the washing machine, no pretending about it.

Balls – For a baby of six months to a child of 10 a ball continues to be a source of great fun. Babies like to roll, touch and chew them, toddlers like to kick, throw and slowly learn to catch them, then comes shared games of football and basketball and complicated against the wall throwing games. They can be inflatable, bouncy, tennis, football, beach, hard, soft or squidgy; all are relatively cheap and can usually survive a great deal of playing and several children.

Puzzles – Simple jigsaw puzzles or peg puzzles can introduce your child to the art of solitary, focused play, which can be a godsend when you need some peace and quiet. What's more, jigsaws also help develop their concentration skills. Jigsaws tend to be fairly cheap to buy and are easily picked up second-hand (but do check all the pieces are there!). As soon as they get too easy, sell them on and replace them.

Games – On a very simple level games can be played from as early as two, for instance matching games with cards (pairs) or picture lotto. Snap is a favourite in our house, too. Later on, you can savour the hours of snakes and ladders and ludo. Games help your child take turns and to share.

Little figures and animals – Lost in an imaginary forest, castle or mountain, children can play for hours with little figures or animals. Such play stimulates their incredible imagination and the possibilities are endless. My son plays with the little animals and submarine men his daddy had when he was a boy as well as the vast collection he has built up over many birthdays and Christmases. He has had hours and hours of fun with these practically indestructible toys, which really are a good investment.

56. FINDING FRIENDS IN THE KNOW

Once you are passed the first baby stage, you need to tap into the best sources of information for the next stage. Your allies in this goal are other full-time mums (and occasionally dads).

Lots of your antenatal group friends may well head back to work when their babies are about 9–12 months old; you may even do some hours yourself. Suddenly your support group can seriously diminish. Don't end up at a loose end, but pal up with like-minded parents. Head out to playgroups, chat to other parents and invite them over or arrange to meet up, just like you did before you started out on this adventure. Things change all the time in the world of babies so view such changes as chances to expand your child's social world and play opportunities – go find some new friends. You need to be just as brave as you were in those antenatal days. Your new friends will probably have a wealth of information to pass on. Perhaps they will know the cheaper, better playgroups, the best parks as well as the budget clothes shops. Stay at home parents are definitely people well worth knowing.

57. THE CHILDCARE CONUNDRUM

If you do return to work your thoughts inevitably turn to childcare. You could choose a childminder, nanny, day nursery, family member or a combination of childcare options. It is a matter of personal preference, availability, convenience and cost. When it comes to childcare, you need to do what is best for your baby, not what is cheapest. You may have a Grandma keen to look after your little treasure for free, but if you don't think it would be the best option then make sure you explore your other options.

Some employers now offer their employees help to pay for childcare. This can include:

- childcare vouchers (see page 267)
- directly contracted childcare
- workplace nurseries.

You can register for childcare vouchers from your pre-tax income provided you are in employment and your employer takes part in a voucher scheme. If your employer doesn't belong to a relevant scheme, encourage them to join one. These vouchers can pay for a broad range of approved childcare (normally that means they have to be registered with Ofsted). As a taxpayer you can save between £962 and £1,196 per year. Do be aware, though, because the money for the vouchers comes out of your income before tax it can affect your level of tax credits. Both you and your partner can take up to a total of £55 per week in vouchers each, so it's a substantial saving.

58. BENEFITS CHECK – ARE YOU GETTING WHAT YOU ARE DUE?

Many of the benefits you're entitled to will change if you return to work, take on some part-time venture or even just because your baby turns one. They may be reduced (for example, child tax credit will go down the more you earn) or stopped completely. Get in touch with your benefits agency and let them know what decisions you have made regarding your work situation so you can update your benefits. You may still receive more than you thought. You don't want to miss out but also you certainly don't want to be overpaid, as you will only have to pay it back. Refer to the section on benefits in the Resource Bank (see page 246) and call the relevant agencies as soon as you have made your decision about work or as soon as your situation changes. It is best to keep up to date.

59. POCKET THE POCKET MONEY

While I have been off with my children, I've been given 50p here and £1 there for my baby. For some strange reason, I would feel duty bound to put all such monies in my children's moneybox where it would sit quietly while I ferreted around the back of the sofa and the depths of my shopping bag for enough change to buy bread. It didn't make any sense. The money was given to my children to make them happy. Me being at home with them made them happy. If I could fund that by buying the groceries then I figured that did make sense. So now, every once in a while, the piggybank coughs up for classes or shopping and I feel totally fine about it. We value the small change given to us and I know my children do, too.

Don't feel money given to your children is untouchable, if you need it then you need it and that really is okay.

CHAPTER 8

Staying Sane Through Those Terrible Twos

Two to three years is a funny old age. Your child needs both roots and wings, and it can be a fine line to tread. Children may desperately want to be independent but just not have the skills or maturity to do things completely by themselves. So, be prepared for a fair amount of frustration and the occasional outburst (from both of you). You don't have to spend money to bribe for good behaviour, there are plenty of free and fabulous things to do that can occupy, challenge and distract your child. Here are some great ideas for surviving those terrible twos and making the absolute best of this fascinating stage of your child's development.

60. EVERYDAY LIFE CAN BE FUN AND FREE (FOR MUMMY'S LITTLE HELPER)

Some say the best things in life are free and as far as young children are concerned this is pretty much always the case. Involve your kids in day-to-day life. Set them in front of the washing machine so they can see the clothes spinning when they are babies, and when they are big enough make a game of sorting out the colours from the whites and then have them load the machine. They can toss the salad ingredients together, help sweep the floor, go to the supermarket...with a little creative thinking you can make all of these things fun. See who can brush the floor the fastest, do household chores to kiddie music, get them to help load the shopping trolley (just watch the eggs!) as you wheel around the supermarket. Life in all its components is interesting and educational for your child, and I've found that boys in particular do well to be involved in domestic life. You never know, their partner may well thank you for it one day.

My little boy, aged five, knows exactly what a bank is for, how to 'pay and display', to make pizza and cakes (out of a packet but who's telling?), to grow vegetables and flowers from seeds, to tidy toys into their proper places and to carry laundry from the washer to the dryer and turn it on. He can make a cup of tea (I pour the hot water!) and he can make his own bed. He can help me sweep the kitchen floor and knows just how to hold the dustpan. Not because I use him as a domestic servant or because I bore him with trivia but because he has been involved in life as I live it since he was born and he thoroughly enjoys it. The majority of his time is play and fun, but he knows about waiting and preparing and has learnt to appreciate what goes into the nice stuff. Hopefully, he won't think the world is there just to entertain him but will know the value of effort and hard work, too.

You don't have to put on entertainment 24/7, it doesn't create a self-reliant child. Babies through to toddlers can find fun in all you do if you make just the slightest effort and talk them through it. It certainly saves a packet on paid entertainment.

61. EMBRACE YOUR ENVIRONMENT

Your environment has lots of free fun to offer you and your child. I live in Nottingham, a city full of contrasts; it is fabulous to have a child here. We have taken our children on walks round Sherwood Forest, boating at the University Lake, for rambles at Colwick Park and bike riding at Sherwood Pines. I took my son to the Warhol exhibition at Nottingham Castle when he was just two. He was terrified by the gorilla at Wollaton Hall but loved the deer. We have had picnics while staring in awe at the canoes speeding down the slalom course at the National Watersports Centre. Frankie has climbed the play castles at Nottingham Castle and he has run through the water fountains in the Old Market Square. He has seen the kite festival at Rushcliffe Country Park and he has ridden up top on double-decker buses. He has made exciting things happen at Greens Mill Science Museum and he has watched the planes take off at East Midlands Airport. He has meandered collecting seeds at Attenborough Nature Reserve. I could go on and on. All these activities were free; and all involved no more than 20 minutes of travelling time.

You may not live in a city but I am sure there will

be fabulous free things to do within half an hour of your home. Read your local newspapers 'What's On' section, ask at the library, look on local noticeboards or check out your nearest tourist information. It's easy to overlook a local wildlife garden centre or city farm if you've never walked past it but if you make an effort to research your locale then the rewards are priceless. Your local environment has much more to offer than you might think, and now you and your toddler can discover it together. It costs nothing more than time and perhaps a packed lunch.

62. MONEY-SAVING MOVIES

On a rainy day a cuddle on the sofa while watching a favourite film is just lovely. When your children are older, having friends over to share that is fun too (I can tell you that little arguing ever occurs when two kids are watching a DVD). You and your parent pals will have a great collection of DVDs between you...so, get sharing, it's far cheaper than buying, or borrow one from the library. Make some popcorn (kids love watching the erratic popcorn try to leap out of the pan) and a jug of squash or water and settle down with some blankets.

Home-made movies are great entertainment too – my son has watched with glee and amazement when seeing himself on the TV. Watching a favourite film is a cosy, quiet, wind-down activity that you can either share with your child or use to keep him occupied while you get some jobs done.

63. DIY CARD MAKING

Before I get onto birthdays (see page 224) I just want to mention cards. In the past, I spent a small fortune on cards. On average, I was spending £1.50 on a piece of card that gets looked at for all of about 30 seconds, stuck on a shelf for a few days then tossed into the recycling bin. I decided that I would save approximately £60 a year on this environmentally unfriendly waste and spend £5 kitting my own little card maker out with all that's needed for DIY cards.

Saving money (and paper) was the motivation for the activity, but since then I have spent hours having fun making cards with my son. He can't get enough of feathers and pasta, stickers and glitter glue, crayons and cut-out pictures from other cards; all such items and more have ended up on his highly original, deeply appreciated cards that have cost mere pennies to produce. Children gain pride, confidence in their artwork and a buzz of creativity from such endeavours – and the feedback from the recipient only boosts such feelings.

Crafts of any kind – whether it be home-made baking, shells stuck on a pot, a pipe cleaner flower or a picture of the sea with foil starfish – make the very best presents for a doting friend or relative. For ideas on craft watch a bit of kids TV, get a book from the library or let your imagination run wild. Get stuck in with your child and enjoy this messy, sticky, gluey time. Come rain or shine, it's a lovely way to spend time together. For some inspiring books check out the Resource Bank (see page 274).

The mess is definitely worth it.

64. GET NATURAL AND GROW YOUR OWN

Growing your own fruit and vegetables is cheap, lots of fun and saves pounds on grocery bills. Last summer, my son and I had a really good crop of onions, some rather straggly tomatoes and some dinky little lettuces to harvest and we were so proud of ourselves. We grew all of them from seed and these seeds were extremely cheap. Not only does he now know how things grow, what they need and the effort required to nurture something, but he also has learned to value the land and even the rain. I want him to love and respect this earth and tend it carefully, so he needs to start learning how. It is his generation who can really get it right and continue what we have started. Another useful concept he is learning is that we can make the things we need, we do not always need to buy them. Garden centres, library books, seed packets and any gardening fanatic neighbours will all tell you what you need to do to get started.

It's best to start small but if your enthusiasm is bursting out, then why not get yourself a family allotment, that way you can probably grow most of your own food. And if you like, you could get chickens in your garden for the eggs. How about a pig or two? Am I getting a bit carried away now? Once you've got the gardening bug, there'll be no holding you back.

65. SAVING THE PLANET, ONE TINY STEP AT A TIME

Consuming less and recycling more are intrinsically linked with saving money, so saving the planet can be a budgeting tip too. Let your children know the environmental value of how you live and, in turn, they will learn to be less materialistic, more resourceful and more creative. As your children's most significant role model, you have to teach them to appreciate and respect their world.

Here are some ideas for inspiring activities you can do to start your child down a good path of caring for their world.

Earth Day

Earth Day began in 1970 in the US and is celebrated on 22nd April each year. It is a day to think about our planet and what we can do to keep it healthy; to think about saving water and energy, reducing pollution, recycling, protecting our animals, trees and plants, and generally getting kids interested in their environment.

Here are my top ideas for celebrating Earth Day with your children.

- Sow some tomatoes or strawberry seedlings or whatever your kids like to eat in your garden or window box
- Put a bowl of water and seeds out for the birds
- Play pooh sticks. Each of you sends a stick over the bridge into the water and race to the other side to see whose comes out first
- Go for a bike ride or a long walk (leave the car behind)
- Hold a nature hunt (send the kids out into the garden or park in teams to find various items on a list you provide)

- Gather family and friends together on a beach or at the park and combine a picnic with a litter pick up
- Get your kids to recycle everything they use on that day: milk bottles, cereal packets, satsuma peel, paper etc. into the right boxes in your home. Let recycling become part of their everyday life
- Have a toy clear out and donate them to your local homeless shelter or charity shop. Do make sure your child selects the toys to go
- Have a party and make it all about the Earth. My friend Sarah and I hosted an Earth Day party at our local park last year and invited about 10 families. They thought we were mad but came along anyway. We did bark rubbings, walked around the park and ate tree-shaped biscuits. We all swapped a book and we planted runner bean seeds in little pots to take home. We had the best of times, spent very little and we were teaching our kids something important

Bookcrossing – join in the fun

Look through your bookshelves and find some books to give away via www.bookcrossing.com. This brilliant idea involves you registering a book you have read online, sticking a little label in it (with a reference number given to you on the site) and then leaving it (yes, that's right) somewhere (a park bench or a café perhaps) for someone else to find it. The finder of your book then registers it online when they've read it and it's passed on and on. If everyone who finds it registers it, you should be able to track its travels – who knows, its journey could span continents. Bookcrossing is a great adventure and a real paper and money saver, too. It is easy to set up and there are no costs involved. I found a Bookcrossing book once and enjoyed a great read for free.

Recycling books

If you aren't online or want to do something that can involve your children, why not donate some of their old books to your local charity shop or library? The Early Learning Centre often runs a 'book amnesty' promotion where you get a discount off new books if you take in a number of old children's books. Even just passing books onto a friend with a younger child is a lovely way to recycle a book and make someone smile.

For other ways to engage your children in saving the planet check out the Resource Bank (page 250).

CHAPTER 9

Taking Care of Yourself (6–36 months post-baby)

Six months after your baby is born you should begin to feel quite human again (hopefully) and remember that the world consists of a bit more than just your baby. You start to think again about that all-important but easily forgotten person – you. If you're like many women who treat themselves by shopping, you'll have to get creative, because for mums on a budget retail therapy is not always possible.

66. BEING GORGEOUS

You may still have the odd broken night of sleep, but hopefully by now your little one is mostly sleeping through the night. So there's no excuse for not getting a good night's sleep. Don't fall into that vicious circle – you look tired and can't be bothered to think about clothes so end up looking scruffy, therefore you feel lacklustre and then can't see the wood for the trees in your wardrobe, so end up wearing the same old outfit.

Instead why not try one or more of my top 10 tips to make the most of your looks without breaking the bank.

RECIPROCAL MANICURES – A manicure can easily cost £20 or more, so save yourself some money but still treat your nails to a bit of tlc. Have a friend do your nails, then when your nail varnish is dry, you can do hers in return. You will both feel a million dollars but won't have spent a single penny. Men, too, have been known to do a great paint job on nails, so ask your partner or husband if he has some free time. To survive looking after a baby, you're best off with clear polish and short tidy nails. But your toes can be transformed in a trice (and they don't get scuffed through nappy changes) and you'll feel über-glamorous in no time.

A SKILL SWAP – Do you have a friend who cuts or colours hair? Perhaps if you're lucky enough to have such a friend, she can do your hair and you can babysit for her in return, or even do her ironing.

GO MOBILE – If hairdresser friends are few and far between, then you can save money by switching from a salon to a mobile hairdresser. Of course, you could always dye your own hair. I have a friend who went back to her natural hair colour after having her baby so she could more easily dye it herself: her locks looked luscious and she saved an absolute fortune. Mobile hairdressers can fit in well with your children, particularly if you are a full-time mum. I always have my hair 'done' as my birthday, Christmas and Mother's day gifts from my husband. It is pricey but it makes me feel fabulous.

GET INTO SHAPE – When you're feeling tired, it's so easy to reach for the biscuit tin, jump in the car instead of walking and flop down on the sofa whenever you get a moment. Try to resist the urge to lounge about, if you feel overweight and unfit this will just make you feel worse. What's stopping you? Running up the stairs, skipping in the garden, riding a bike and walking to the shops and park are all free – plus, you'll look and feel better for some endorphin-releasing activity.

DITCH THE JUNK FOOD – Eat simple, healthy meals and shun the sugar-filled nibbles – not only are they sending your blood sugar on a rollercoaster ride, they're expensive too.

NATURE'S PLAYGROUND – Get lots of fresh air: it does wonders for your skin and makes you feel energised; what's more, if you take baby along too, the daylight exposure can help them sleep well at night. (It's easy to remember your baby's SPF and easy to forget yours, choose an SPF of 15 or more.)

SORT THOSE HAIRS OUT – Someone's got to say it! Your bikini line may well have been abandoned during pregnancy but now you can see it again you really should do something about it. While you're there, tidy up your eyebrows and sort out any hairy armpits or legs. These looks may be low maintenance but, if you took care of these areas before and don't now, you could end up feeling untidy and possibly unsexy. Of course, there's nothing wrong with embracing the hairy look if it's one you love.

GET SOME EXCELLENT BASICS – You won't be able to spend money on clothes like you used to, and now practicality is key. But, whatever you wear, you can still be clean and stylish. Leggings and a plain white t-shirt always look good, with comfy but hardwearing shoes (I live in my Converse – they're worth every penny and wash well too). Jeans and a good pair of boots are another ideal pairing. Once you've found the jeans for you, you can wear them endlessly – dressed down with a cosy jumper or glammed up with a satin or sparkly top. Accessories update your look – a new bag or hairband in this season's colours can make you look bang on trend for little cost.

A GOOD SKIN CARE ROUTINE – It's all too easy to neglect your own skin care when you are a busy mum with someone else's face to wash, teeth to clean, etc. So, at the least, aim to cleanse and moisturise your skin once a day. Having a good skin care routine combined with fresh air, eating well and drinking water are all key components to looking good. (If you want a little extra help a tube of lip gloss can go a long way, takes mere seconds to apply and can cost very little. I always keep one in my bag!)

THE MAGICAL POT OF VASELINE – If you are going to buy one beauty item, make sure it's Vaseline. You can style your eyebrows with it, put it on your cheekbones, use it as a hand and foot cream and, of course, as lip gloss. Vaseline is cheap, cheerful and the small pots fit in your handbag (and can even double as nappy cream). Give your cheeks a pinch for some colour and use an old toothbrush to brush those eyebrows. Tell yourself loud and proud: you are gorgeous!

Ultimately, I know none of the above matters; being happy and healthy is most important in life. But it is true that looking good can make you feel good, and when it's affordable, why not?

67. SHARING LIFE'S LITTLE LUXURIES

Share and you will be shared with is, I believe, a true maxim. A friend of mine saves her magazines each and every month for me. What a treat. I read them and pass them onto another friend who gives them, after she has read them, to her sister-in-law. Magazines are a luxury and sharing maximises their use – so everyone gets a slice. If you show you are willing to share, people seem to understand it is okay to pass on to you, too, without you being offended.

68. SKILL SHARING

If you can cut hair and your friend is a card-making wizard then arrange a trade off. If you bake a mean birthday cake and they can sew a straight hem, then there are sharing opportunities to be explored. If you can offer babysitting in lieu of car repairs to a mechanic mate, then you can cut out the need for money altogether.

My husband is a wonderful and friendly IT guy (of course, I'm biased). In return for his IT services, we have received, among other things: free car maintenance, crystals, wine, the decoration of our entire house, chocolate, meals out, beauty treatment discounts, cottage holidays and pretty much a complete loft conversion. He has saved us a fortune.

Although skill sharing can't always be like for like in terms of cost, try to make sure it's not way off. For example, if you are given a cast-off pair of wellies for your son don't feel you have to do a five-hour babysit in return. Offering to walk their dog or giving some daffodils from your garden would be a lovely gesture and definitely enough.

69. GIFTS WORTH GETTING

As you have by now got into the habit of speaking up about your children's preferred gifts, don't forget it can apply to you too. Treat times, such as birthdays and Christmas, are precious but you also want something substantial and not a piece of expensive jewellery you dare not wear around kids. Ask for what you'd really like – a year's subscription to a magazine or some beauty treatment vouchers, a couple of books or a gym membership (well, we can dream can't we?). But seriously, speak up. You could even ask for money. On occasions, I've needed to use gift money to take care of the bills, and while this might seem a shame, the peace of mind it brought made it completely worthwhile.

If your partner wants to give you something special but has a very limited budget, you could always ask for a day off parenting. What could be more lovely than a lie-in, a bubble bath, breakfast in bed with your favourite magazine or book? It costs nothing to give but feels totally indulgent to receive.

70. 'ME TIME' FOR NEXT TO NOTHING

I bet you don't get much time to just be by yourself any more, so indulge yourself and take some time out to remind yourself who you are.

A BIG LAZY BATH – This practically free and gorgeous luxury should relax and revitalise you. Unplug the phone, warm up your towel on the radiator, pop on your favourite music, light a few candles, sip your glass of wine and, aaaaaaaah, relax. Save your top-to-toe beauty routine (shaving, plucking, exfoliating, etc.) for shower days. On bath day, it's pure indulgence.

SKY+ SAVVY – Set your Sky+ box or your HD recorder so that you never miss a single episode of your favourite TV shows. That way, you'll always have something great to watch at the flick of a button.

MUSICAL MAESTRO – Make housework less of a chore by singing along (or dancing) to your favourite music. Babies do not need silence to sleep, so don't worry about waking them up. Music is a great mood enhancer – it can make you feel energised or help you to chill out, whichever you need.

BORROW A GOOD BOOK – Set your children a great example by reading for pleasure (though you'd be lucky to get more than 10 minutes at a time during the day) or just enjoy a story while you soak in the bath. It'll cost you nothing more than the trip to the library.

WALK IN WONDERLAND – Head to places where you like to walk and soak up all its wondrous beauty – you kids will be happy to tag along.

MAKE A DATE TO SEE AN EXHIBITION – Don't miss out on a must-see event. Children can be lovely companions as they see through fresh eyes.

DIAL A FRIEND – Set your child up with an activity and call your best friend for a natter, read that book you got out of the library or have a lovely coffee in peace in the next room. As long as they are safe and stimulated children do not need entertaining 24/7. I aim for some 'me time' like this maybe twice a day. It's good for us all and is totally free.

MAKE YOUR WORLD BEAUTIFUL – Arrange some flowers from the garden in a vase or cut out an inspiring article from a magazine and stick it on the fridge. Take a minute to write and tell your Great Aunt she is special, close your eyes and listen to your favourite track, stare at a sunset or take up t'ai chi in the serenity of an early morning. Nurture your life, don't let parenting be everything. Simple, free, lovely little moments can keep your soul full and spirit soaring, without the need for an expensive spa day.

GET OUT OF THE HOUSE –Whether it's for a coffee and the paper *sans* toddlers on a Saturday morning, a walk in the park without holding a hand or a cup of tea with a friend, sometimes we just need to be without our kids; no guilt, no fuss, just refreshing time away.

RELAX AND CHILL OUT – Learn to meditate or take up pilates, anything that helps maximise relaxation and dissolve stress. Inner peace may be the only peace you will get, so you need to learn how to access it fast. My friend Nikki took a salsa class. It was, as she expected, madly energetic but she also found she truly relaxed and forgot all about her normal life as she danced. Rather than feeling exhausted she felt totally uplifted and calm. Trying something new can totally change your mood.

You don't have to spend a fortune, just don't neglect yourself or life as a mum on a budget will feel much, much harder.

71. READ ALL ABOUT IT!

It's vital to keep up to date with the world around you, not only does it keep your mind active but also stops your world from feeling so small. And, there's only so long you can talk about babies – your friends (and partner) will thank you for a change in conversation.

If you don't want to fork out for a daily paper, or can't go to the library every day, then make the most of your free local papers. You will find out what's going on locally and you can often get TV listings there too.

An update on world events can be had at the flick of

a switch on the radio or TV. What's more, you can now access news whenever you like via 24-hour news channels or via the Internet and while you're there, check out the good old gossip. For a selection of the best free Internet resources check out the Resource Bank (page 253).

72. BARGAIN HOLIDAYS

At this point in your life as a new parent you may be desperate for a holiday but completely unable to afford one. It is important to have a break from routine. New scenery recharges your batteries and gives you fresh perspectives. And you'll all get to spend time together as a family. Think about what you want most from your holiday and try to be creative. If you yearn for the seaside, think about any friends who live near the coast who you can visit or arrange a house swap with. For a countryside setting, hiring a cottage out of season is cheaper than you think (as long as it's outside school holidays). If you want hands-on activities without paying a fortune, look into sharing a stay at Center Parcs with another family or some friends; off-peak and self-catered, such a break can be exceptional value.

If you crave some sun and your budget can stretch to overseas look out for last-minute bargains online and on Teletext. The more last minute and flexible you can be the more likely you are to bag a deal. A foreign holiday may sound expensive, but just bear in mind that three days at a rainy British seaside can cost you more than a package holiday to Spain off-season, because you'll be paying for endless entertainment.

Don't be tempted to shop for a holiday wardrobe. For this holiday at least, you can surely make do with what you have. I mean, apart from your partner and your baby, the only people who will get to appreciate your new threads are strangers who you will probably never see again.

Credit-crunch camping

Don't overlook the simple – and purse-friendly – pleasures of camping and caravanning; over the past few years camping has become cool again and there are plenty of guidebooks (see page 248). My pal Sarah takes her little boy camping each summer, sometimes with other families too. She bought their tent and bits and bobs for about £150 and their holidays are now cheap and lots of fun. They spend hours in the fresh air and can just decide to pack up and go any weekend the weather is nice. Another friend took her son to a Eurocamp in France and had a fantastic budget holiday.

I remember caravan holidays at Skegness when I was a child with my grandparents and I have lovely memories of flip flops, sand, ice cream and playing cards. Last year, my family went to Mablethorpe on a caravan holiday – it was a cosy home-from-home right near the beach and the accommodation cost less than £100 for the week.

Try something different, it may be out of your comfort zone but a night under the stars or in a caravan by the sea are the stuff of memories. Plenty of my friends remember such childhood holidays with great fondness and always have some tale or other to tell.

73. GIVE YOURSELF A 'FEEL GOOD' FIX FOR FREE

A free and fabulous way to feel good is to create a gratitude journal. Admittedly, I've borrowed this idea from Gwyneth Paltrow on Oprah. Gwynnie told Oprah how each day she writes down three things she is grateful for that happened that day. Whenever she is feeling even slightly down a glance back though her journal makes her smile. Sometimes having little money can make us feel a bit low. In the past, you might well have nipped down the shops for a quick pick-me-up or had a night out to cheer yourself up. But now you don't have that kind of spare cash you need to find other ways to do this. Gratitude journals are a really positive way to lift your mood and keep you grounded. It is good for us to remember the value of every day. Get yourself a beautiful book and write down your three good things each and every day; and look at your book whenever you are doubtful. Gwyneth seems to be doing all right; check out www.goop.com for other great lifestyle tips from Ms Martin herself.

Continue your focus on good things and encourage your child (when he's older) at bedtime to name three great things to give thanks for. How fantastic to end the day on such a positive note.

Feeling good needn't cost money, a positive attitude and a dose of gratitude is all you really need.

74. DON'T SHOP IT, SWAP IT!

Swap It parties are not about throwing in your keys to find a new partner or about exchanging your trying toddler for a well-behaved little angel. They are, in fact, a fabulous idea that is green, friendly and great if you are skint.

Oxfam champion what they call Swap It parties, which encourage people to host gatherings, where people bring 'stuff', swap 'stuff' and then take anything left over to their local Oxfam shop.

According to Oxfam, in the UK we throw away enough to fill the Royal Albert Hall every two hours. And, shockingly, 90 per cent of what we buy ends up in landfill within six months. Such levels of consumption only accelerate climate change and are pushing the poorest in society further into poverty. Oxfam hopes that these parties will not only inspire people to consume in a fun, creative way, but will also create a space for people to discuss the impact we're having on the planet.

All you need to do for a Swap It party is:

- have a big clear-out and pile together everything you no longer want
- invite your friends over for a Swap It evening, telling them to bring along any items they no longer want (to keep things simple, you may want a theme, such as children's toys or women's clothes or you may be happy to have anything)
- put out a few nibbles (friends can bring some too) and clear lots of space
- arrange the items around the room so they can easily be seen
- invite everyone to take whichever items they want (providing labelled bags with people's names may be a good idea).

Once everyone's happy with their non-purchases, why not reinforce Oxfam's message by watching its video on climate change and start your own discussion, followed by a good old natter. Whatever form your party takes, you are doing your bit for the planet and saving money.

Swap It parties offer you a chance to declutter and get some great new items (oh no, does that count as clutter?) along the way. Go to www.oxfam.co.uk/get_involved/campaign/activists/swapit.html where you can download invites, product labels, a video and much, much more.

CHAPTER 10

The Pre-School Years (3–5)

While you're at home with your little one, what can you do to make sure that he or she is well stimulated, healthy and properly prepared for school, as well as out from under your feet occasionally? Well, read on. This chapter has a wealth of ideas on how to keep both your child entertained and you sane, while always considering that all-important budget.

75. EARLY EDUCATION SESSIONS ARE FREE

Did you know that from the age of three every child is entitled to 12½ hours of free childcare a week? The Pre-School Learning Alliance offers the following information on free educational placements for three- to five-year-olds:

All three and four year olds are entitled to a free part-time early education place. This means your child will be eligible for five 2½ hour sessions of free education a week, for 38 weeks a year. The part-time

*places are available in school nursery classes, state
or private nursery schools, day nurseries, pre-schools
and with accredited childminders who are part of a
quality assured network.*

*Local authorities use the following nationally prescribed dates
for determining eligibility for this free entitlement.*

A child born on or between	Will become eligible for a free place from
1 April and 31 August	1 September following their third birthday
1 September and 31 Dec	1 January following their third birthday
1 January and 31 March	1 April following their third birthday

By 2010, plans are in place for 15 hours of free education
to be available each week. The 15 hours will be flexible,
offering parents the option to access five hours for
three days, or three hours for five days. Different local
authorities are starting this at different times, so do check
with yours. For more details on this check out www.pre-
school.org.uk.

Parents can use their free sessions in a variety of ways.
My son had two sessions a week at a pre-school playgroup
that took three- to four-year-olds for 2½ hour morning
sessions. He also had two sessions at a day nursery that
provided pre-school places. Again this placement was for
just 2½ hours but with options to stay for lunch, mix with
younger children, etc. So, I used only 10 hours a week
of my 12½ hour entitlement. When he reached four, I

dropped to just two 2½ sessions a week because school was looming and I wanted to spend more time with him.

In terms of administration, both the playgroup and the nursery sorted out the payment with the government, all I had to do was signs some forms. They arranged it all. I have a friend whose son is in nursery three full days a week and she has these free 12½ hours deducted from her bill, while another friend uses her hours with a childminder.

Pre-schools and playgroups – what are they?

Pre-schools offer the chance for children to play and learn in an age-appropriate group setting usually for a 2½ hour session either in a morning or in an afternoon. Places usually start from two-and-a-half to three years, and continue up to school age. Some are attached to schools and some are held in church halls or other independent buildings. They are sometimes organised by the community on a not-for-profit basis, often with the help of parents. Pre-schools are registered by the government regulatory bodies and are inspected every year by Ofsted. Half the staff must be trained and some may be qualified teachers. They'll offer lots of opportunities for children to learn through play, and most offer a government-approved early years' curriculum. Playgroups are very similar, though may be more informal. If registered, playgroups are also Ofsted inspected. Children love to spend time together and it is a nice little break for you too. Check out www.surestart.gov.uk for more information on pre-schools and playgroups.

Your local Children's Information Service (CIS) can also advise you on childcare options and availability in your area. The CIS provides impartial advice and guidance on childcare, early education and other children's services. They hold information on Ofsted-registered childcare such as day nurseries, out-of-school clubs, pre-school playgroups and childminders, as well as unregistered settings where children get together, such as parent-and-toddler groups. You can get the telephone number of your nearest CIS by calling 0800 234 6346. All Ofsted inspection reports are available online at www.ofsted. gov.uk.

For more contact information please see the Resource Bank (page 255).

76. A LOVE OF LEARNING STARTS AT HOME

You don't have to pay out for nurseries or pre-schools to ensure your child is prepared for school. Your own teaching is more than good enough. Your child has been learning from you from the second they were born: how to smile, walk, talk, even use the toilet – yet suddenly when it comes to learning letters and numbers, it's all too easy to panic. Teaching your child the basics of letters and numbers is easy to do, but it is a good idea to research current teaching options (such as phonics for letters) so that your child doesn't have to unlearn anything when he gets to school. A 1:1 ratio, teaching your child yourself (rather than the 1:8 in a pre-school or nursery), has many advantages. Here's how I did it.

Every Wednesday throughout his toddler years my son and I went out for an early walk round the park and breakfast. Each week we bought a children's magazine from the newsagents next to the coffee shop and sat and read it, doing all the activities, as we ate our toasted teacakes (his favourite). He loved this weekly event and it really helped him learn as we attempted the different letter and number games using familiar characters and fun scenarios – and there were always lots of stickers awards (CBeebies magazine was always his top choice).

Frankie also learned his numbers playing skittles, putting magnetic numbers on the fridge, counting his toys and singing songs like '12345, Once I caught a fish alive' and 'Three little men in a flying saucer'. Other ways he learned numbers included counting books from the library, adding up how many red cars we spotted on a journey and how many coins he had in his moneybox. I let him pay for items in shops and we played shops at home, too, with a cash till. We built our learning into our everyday life, nothing too structured or clever, just basic stuff we did together, which he enjoyed.

Frankie learnt his letters through *Chicka Chicka Boom Boom*, read again and again and again. (If you haven't read this book it's an American classic and we love it to bits in our house.) In addition to that, he has foam letters (bought very cheaply from a supermarket) we play with in the bath and stick onto the tiles. We practised writing his names and saying 'f' is for fish, 'r' is for robot, etc. All this letter learning took place over time, through play and normal life and with no real expense. Children learn naturally if exposed to enough material, so just keep facilitating this and their learning will most probably fall into place.

For a list of great educational and fun resources check out the Resource Bank (see page 273), but don't forget the free and natural world around you offers plenty of opportunities.

77. PLAYING GAMES AND SAVING POUNDS

Toys cost money, and going to playcentres, swimming pools and the like, despite being fun, can seriously dent your purse. So, rediscover the world of good, old-fashioned, free game playing. From about the age of three, children are able to play more sophisticated games and it is a great way for them to learn simple turn-taking and basic rules.

I have spent many hours playing hide and seek, building a tent for teddies, playing snap and snakes and ladders, kicking a football in the garden and having pretend tea parties. I have helped my son wash dollies and put all the toy cars in colour order then size order, I have told hundreds of made up Pingu stories and I have had races up and down our garden, again and again and again. I have played pairs, ludo and simple board games and helped Frankie play many games on the computer.

Playing games with your child is fantastic fun and a great way to teach them co-operation as well as many other skills, such as counting, spatial awareness and fairness. It requires little equipment, just a few odd toys or bits and bobs. For example, 'Let's see how fast you can put all those items into piles of whites and colours' is a very useful washing game I know and have exploited many times. Energy, creativity and a willingness to follow their lead are all it takes to play.

Board games can be pricey but you can often get them second-hand at charity shops or at nursery or school fairs. If you want something specific, explore eBay.

Here are my top 10 games to play with your pre-schooler that won't cost you a penny.

1. Hide and seek

Get them to count to 10 if they can and run and hide. (If they can't count that far then have them shut their eyes while you count for them, then shout 'Come and get me!') Make it easy to start with and become more creative as they gain confidence. Take it in turns to be the seeker and the hider. Stick to places you know – I prefer to play this game indoors or in the garden rather than an enormous park. This game is great for counting, creativity and patience skills (don't make them search for too long, though). I have childhood memories of once hiding in an upright laundry basket, no one finding me after ages and having to throw myself on the floor to get out and getting a bit bruised in the process. Be sure to tell your child what is off limits, for instance not going inside washing machines or in the compost bin. Be sure to make lots of noise if they aren't looking in the right area and shout 'Boo!' really loudly when they find you.

2. Snap and pairs

You and your child can easily make your own snap cards. Cut up lots of rectangular card (of the same colour) into pieces about the size of a standard playing card. Decide what objects you want on them, it could be all animals, shapes or characters from a story or TV show. Now make a pair of cards that match, then move on to the rest. You could use glitter, stickers (two packs the same), even painted fingerprints; the idea is to make them as fun and appealing as possible but remember that the pairs need to be identical so don't go over the top.

Playing snap

To play snap (in case you've forgotten!), shuffle your pack of cards and deal them out so you each have the same number of cards. Each player in turn puts down a card face up on the top of the card that has already been put down. If two sequential cards match, the first player to say 'Snap!' and put their hand on top of the card wins the pile. They simply add these cards to the bottom of their pile. The player with all the cards at the end is the winner.

Snap is great for encouraging concentration, turn-taking and learning how to be a good loser because even the most uncompetitive mummy can't help yelling 'Snap!' if she spots it first.

Playing pairs

First, spread out your cards on a smooth surface (not all of them, just perhaps eight to start with) making sure each card has an exact match. Put them plain side up and have your child turn one over and then another to see if they match. If they do match, your child keeps the pair and has another go. If they don't match, put them back in the same place and you have a go at finding two of a kind. The winner is the player who has the most pairs.

3. Treasure hunt

Frankie was completely hassling me one day while I was trying to have a chat on the phone so I said 'Go and find me a green tennis ball' and he was back two minutes later, delighted with himself, ball in hand saying, 'What shall I find now mummy?' Our treasure hunt game was born. I make a long list of about 15 items, some easy to find some not so easy, and send him off to find them one by one.

Items on the list might include:

- a book with an animal picture on it
- a newspaper
- a shoe
- one of his sister's nappies (clean!)
- a sock
- a cuddly toy
- a remote control
- a pillow

An alternative list for an outdoors version of this game might include:

- a big leaf
- a little leaf
- a yellow flower

- a stone
- a plastic plant pot
- a twig
- a watering-can
- a nice chilled glass of wine and some snacks (Ha! In my dreams)

Hunting for treasure is great fun with a friend too. Get them to find things together rather than make it competitive, it saves a lot of arguing and fosters teamwork. A little juice and snack is a great 'prize' for finding all the items.

4. Guess what?

To keep your child entertained if you are stuck on a bus, in a doctors' waiting room or just about anywhere, all you need is a scrap of paper and a pen. Frankie and I play the Guess what? game a lot. I start drawing and he has to guess what I am drawing. He can stop me at any time or I will pause at various points and ask him to guess what he thinks the picture is. Sheep, houses, trees, birds all look like lots of other things if you just do one shape at a time, A cloud shape can become a tree or a sheep or even a ladies hairdo. A triangle can become a roof or a tent. Such games can offer a great distraction and help children to sit still for a while.

A variation of this game involves making your body into a position or doing an action and asking your child to 'Guess who?' you are; for example, a crossing warden, a postman, a gardener or a builder. You may need to add sound effects and more movements if he gets stuck.

5. Taste testing

For this game you will need a soft blindfold and various food items. Only blindfold your child if he is okay with it then get him to taste different things and guess what they are; have a pen and paper on hand to write down the answers next to the foodstuff. Afterwards, he can have great fun finding out what he was really tasting. Chocolate, ketchup, ice cream and apple puree are all good things to use. But don't get children to try mustard – it'll put them off food tasting games forever. If your child has a friend over, be sure to check with their parents about any allergies before playing this game.

We've had such laughs with this game, but it's also great for linking tastes to names, trying out new tastes and generally making food fun. You can always add a bit of extra information as you go – 'What do you think crisps are made from?', 'What vegetable is in ketchup?' and so on.

6. Skittles

Whether you knock down tin cans with a tennis ball or plastic plant pots with a football in the garden, skittles can provide hours of free fun. Inside, you can knock over little cuddly toys or plastic cups with a softer ball instead. The players decide whether the balls are kicked, rolled or thrown, and you take it in turns or keep going until one player has knocked them all down, then the next person has a go. You can use this game to enhance counting skills (How many down? How many left?) and turn-taking.

7.What's missing?

Memory games are fun and simple to set up. Put six familiar items on a tray and have your children look at them carefully. Tell them you are going to take one away and have them go out of the room while you do so. See if they can spot what's gone. If they get it right, they get a big tick on the score sheet. Keep going till they have four ticks. (Hint: if they aren't getting any then maybe you have too many items on your tray.)

Another version involves putting toys, one by one, into an empty box while your child watches. Then, put a blanket on top and ask your child to shout out any toy they can remember seeing going into the box. As they guess correctly, slip your hand under the blanket and pull out the toy. See if he or she can empty the whole box. Give them one tick for each toy remembered. Play this memory game when they have friends over, as between them they will remember most of the toys.

8. Hotter...colder...

Who hasn't played this game? Basically you hide something and set your child the task of finding it. You shout out 'hot', 'hotter' and 'hotter still' as they get nearer to the object and 'cold', 'colder' and 'freezing cold' when they are miles off. Children love this game and will want to play it again and again. Why not get yourself a cup of tea, grab a seat on the sofa and relax while they play?

9. Balloon pop

Most kids adore balloons (but if your child has a fear of bangs from balloons then steer clear of this one) and this is a balloon game with a twist. Place notes inside uninflated balloons, with different instructions written on them, for example Jump five times or Kiss your mummy or Sing 'Jack and Jill'; anything simple, achievable and familiar. Once inside, blow up the balloons and let your child pop them. Once popped, he or she has to hand you the note and you reveal the special instruction. When all balloons are popped, it's time for a snack and a drink as your little one will be shattered. Such games are great for wearing children out (balloons can take ages to pop if you don't know how) and having them follow simple instructions.

10. I spy

I spy is great for developing observational skills and developing vocabulary. I am sure that everyone knows how to play, but just in case it has been a while since you played, here is a quick recap. Obviously this game requires at least two players. You need to look around and think of an object that all players can (easily) see. You then say, 'I spy with my little eye something beginning with...' and then the first letter of the word. With little kids it is best to use the phonetic sound of the letter and give some extra description, for example, 'I spy something beginning with b... that sometimes we travel on to get into town.' If your children are really young you may want to miss out the letter completely and just give a description, for instance, 'I spy…something red with four wheels that carries people and travels on the road.' Let the player who correctly guesses the word pick the next object, or have all players take turns in a set order (this may be best if you are playing with younger children who may not be so good at guessing). Younger children may find it a bit tough to be the describer but just let them keep guessing for as long as it's fun.

78. SOCIAL LIFE AND SLEEPOVERS

As your child gets older, he or she'll start to ask for friends to come over and play or, often, to invite themselves over to their friends' houses. Prepare yourself for your child's hectic social life. This preparation needn't mean saving up for expensive playdates, but it will require some courage on your part. In the pre-school years, friends start to come to play without their parents. The thought of the playdate may well prove worse than the actuality, since the two of them will pretty much amuse themselves and so give you some free time, apart from the obligatory drinks and snacks. All you need to do is get out the toys. Invite only those children you know well and who your child gets on well with. Their mummy may well be your 'best friend' but it doesn't follow that your children will be best friends, too. Don't force friendships, go with who your child likes and follow their lead.

Kids seem to ask for sleepovers from such a young age now, but just because they're asking for them doesn't mean they're ready for them. Sleepovers can be a huge success but if you think your child is up to sleeping at a friend's house, and if you're hosting one don't expect the kids to go to sleep at their normal time. If other parents offer to have your child to sleepover, be sure you know and trust them completely and your child feels very safe and wants to go. Don't ever feel you have to agree to an invitation just to be polite. There will be plenty of years ahead for this sort of activity.

79. DITCH THE CAR

It is fantastically good for you to go out walking or cycling and it is free. It is so sad we are rapidly raising a nation of increasingly obese children who seem to spend far too much time watching TV, playing on computers or on the playstation. Resolve not to take the car everywhere you go and walk or cycle wherever possible. What's more, car journeys equal petrol costs. Take a stand against pollution and childhood obesity and save yourself some money too – leave the car at home!

A two-minute trip back from pre-school in the car also gives you far less time to find out about what your child has been up to than a 20-minute amble home. Think how good natural, sociable exercise is for you both. Not only will you save money, but you'll also strengthen your bond and keep yourselves fit. Making walking or cycling a part of everyday life teaches them good life habits. It does take more time to walk or cycle about, but time is something you usually have if you're not working.

Once they are big enough, invest in a scooter, trike or

pedal-free bike to get little legs moving fast (which speeds up journeys), and brings them endless pleasure. Bikes can be well looked after and so buying second-hand is a great idea. You can always buy a few little add-ons – a bell with a favourite character on or some tassles on the handlebars – to personalise it.

If you really get into walking with your child it may become much more than just a form of travel and blossom into a lovely activity that you enjoy together. Walking can be fabulous fun: along the sides of canals, up hills, over rocky paths, by the sea, around lakes and even just through fields. Children soon catch the walking bug and once their interest is piqued all whines about tired legs fade away to 'Wow! Look at that.'

For books on walks suitable for children around the country and for details of cheap family-friendly walking holidays check out the Resource Bank (page 257).

80. LET YOUR CHILD LEAD

It's easy to become fed up with activities if you're always the one initiating what you're going to do today. So, why not ask your child to be in charge once in a while? Children from the age of three are capable of increasing independence. They like to take the lead and make decisions for themselves; it can mean the world to them. Their imagination is bursting, so take advantage of this untapped pool of ideas. Now, when you have a picnic your child can help decide what to take, they can help make the food (keep it simple), choose the activities and even help decide where to have it. Encouraging this independence means that they get so much more enjoyment from it, knowing they've participated and taken some control.

Pizza-making, cake-baking, paying your fare on a bus, cleaning the car, painting a wall, helping to hang out the washing, planting some seeds, bathing their baby sister, even polishing the bookshelf can all be fun for a three-year-old as they can work alongside you. Give them their library card and get them to check out their own books at the library. Asking them to help you write a shopping list can make them feel important and develop essential life skills, as well as adding much more fun to day-to-day jobs you do. Every activity can be fun for a pre-schooler, and their imagination and independence will soar as they play.

Keep doing what you do already, with more freedom and room for imagination. Your child will naturally grow and expand his skills. My five-year-old spent two hours cleaning my car and had the time of his life. The car was both streaky and gleamy at the same time but he had a ball. He was very proud of himself.

81. MUSIC (MAKING IT UP AND MAKING YOUR OWN)

Music is vital to a child's development. It is fun, mood changing, teaches rhythm, supports speech development, helps memory, co-ordination, brain development and relaxation, to name a few. It is also extremely accessible so need not involve much expense. Children love music of all kinds – whether it's on the radio, on a CD in the car, on your iPod playlist or live right in front of them. In Nottingham, where I live, the John Lewis department store hosts 'Beanbag Proms' – classical music shows for little kids. Such concerts are great fun and are often free. Check out if there is anything similar in your neck of the woods.

With either very little or no cost, my son has played on steel drums at community events, he has line-danced with me at an American Music Festival and we have swirled and twirled in the kitchen to the radio. We have sung 'Humpty Dumpty' a million times on the side of the swimming pool and his nursery rhyme CDs for the car should be worn out they've been played so much. We have sung in the bath together and done actions as necessary, as in all the little ducks swimming away. He has sung gently to his little sister all the songs I sang to him as a baby. At gymnastics we have enthusiastically acted out lots of movement songs. We have made instruments out of bits and bobs, and we have made up silly songs too.

All sorts of music become accessible to small children if you approach it with enthusiasm and join in. My mum even got Frankie to enjoy and request 'Country Christmas songs' in her car but I am sure sweetie bribes must have been involved. You don't have to go to a baby music class to introduce your little one to music and song, and you'll do well to play him a range of music, not just the kiddie nursery rhymes. Have fun with music – all music. It is the start of a lifelong love affair that need cost very little. YouTube has provided us with many prolonged breakfasts with the children watching Songs from Nemo while I wash up as well as many hours of kitchen dancing, too!

Go to sleep my baby…

I was given a book when my son was born that told me about the Mbuti of Zaire who sing lullabies to their babies that are composed purely for a newborn by their mother. They are sung for no other and by no other, ever. In the same spirit I made up simple little secret songs for both my children and they smile when I sing their songs to them. Lullabies have a slow steady beat that echoes an adult's heartbeat and so children of all ages relax to them as they confer messages of safety and comfort.

Shake, rattle and roll

Making and shaking instruments can be terrific fun and home-made versions cost nothing. Put some pasta in a box and, hey presto, it's a rattle; elastic bands over a tissue box make an instant guitar; or just drum fingers or bash a wooden spoon on an upside-down washing-up bowl. Let you hair down and have some fun with instruments and your child will, too. GG (Great Grandma) put some rice in an empty cod-liver oil tub three years ago; this little tub has been a big hit with all four of her great grandchildren and is still going strong.

Learning the words

To find some great nursery rhymes and action songs raid your local library for books and CDs. Kids TV shows such as the Tweenies always have lots of action songs in them and the CBeebies website (www.cbeebies.co.uk) is another great store of songs with the words given on the site.

Get on down at the disco, baby

You do have to pay to go to a baby disco (about £5 per person) but they are fantastic value for money and once you've got the general the idea you can always throw open your doors and recreate your own version at home.

Baby discos are becoming increasingly popular with parents and toddlers who want to party. Typically a nightclub is hired for an afternoon and mums, dads and their tots get to dance. Boogie babies (www.boogie.moonfruit.com) who organise such events in the Midlands describe their sessions as follows:

The DJ plays feel-good tunes to get the grown ups and little ones dancing and moving, and we make the most of the disco lights and glitter balls of the nightclub! We have balloons to enjoy, play scarves and a chill-out space with pillows, tents and books.

It's still quite a new concept but check out the Resource Bank (page 241) to see if there are any baby discos near you. If not, maybe you could hire a nightclub and organise one!

82. EXERCISE AND PLAY THE OLD-FASHIONED WAY

For most children, running and playing actively are as natural as breathing. While it can be tempting for parents to encourage their children to sit quietly (all of that noise and activity can be trying at times), it is far better to allow and even promote children's innate desire to move their bodies. Childhood obesity is at an all-time high, but parents who provide their little ones with a healthy diet and plenty of opportunities for active play give their children the best possible start in life. Active children are learning to love exercise, and that's a great lesson.

Entertaining games needn't cost the earth and ones that benefit them physically are even better. Try out any of the following games, all taken from a great website (www.kidsexercise.co.uk). These games are suitable for pre-schoolers but I reckon that both younger and older children would still have fun with them – they are spot on for parties, too.

Duck, duck, goose

In this traditional game, children sit in a circle with one child standing outside of the circle. The standing child walks around the circle, tapping the heads of friends while saying 'duck' to each child. Then, while tapping the head of their chosen friend, the walker says 'goose' rather than 'duck'. The chosen child has to spring up off the floor and run around the circle, trying to tag the child who tapped them before that child can sit down in the free spot in the circle. The game continues, with each child taking a turn.

Musical chairs

A series of chairs is set up in a line, typically with one less than the number of children playing. A parent plays music and instructs the kids to walk around the chairs until the music stops, after which the children have to find themselves a chair to sit on as quickly as they can. Whichever child fails to locate a chair sits out and another chair is removed, so that the game can continue in the same way. Play continues until one child secures the last remaining chair. A non-competitive version of this game can be played by substituting hoops on the ground and then instructing the children to leap inside a hoop (they can share space) every time the music stops.

Ball toss

Children gather into a circle, either outdoors or in a large, open area. Someone tosses a lightweight ball (a beach ball works very well) into the mix of children, who are supposed to try to keep the ball in the air for as long as possible. Children are usually happy to play this game repeatedly, attempting to improve the time that they can keep the ball off the floor.

Follow the leader

In this game, children take turns leading their friends through a series of movements (walking, skipping, running, hopping, etc.). Most children love to be the leader but enjoy it anyway when the leader chooses particularly silly moves for the group to imitate.

Tag

Most adults played games of tag as children, and it is enjoyed today as much as ever. One child is designated as 'it' and chases the other children until one is tagged. That child then becomes 'it' and the game continues.

ABCs and 1-2-3s

Children use their bodies to form the shapes of letters and numbers that are called out to them, stretching and bending as needed. When several children work together to form the shapes, giggles are sure to follow.

It is worth encouraging your child to play hard and exercise. Be sure to keep fit yourself (see page 120 for some low-cost ideas). Children need to see you value and respect your body and they need to see activity as a regular, natural, fun part of life. You are their best and most important role model. They do what you do far more than what you tell them to do.

83. CREATE YOUR OWN PERFECT GROUP

Library sing-alongs and other such free children's activities are often for the under-threes and yet three- to five-year-olds have so much energy and, of course, they need age-appropriate activities too.

I know a woman who regularly met with other parents and their kids but found her house could not contain them all. This group of active under-fives needed space to run around, big tables to do crafts and have snacks, room to set up huge train sets and make-believe houses. As a group these parents often went along to mother-and-toddler sessions but found their more boisterous, older kids were a bit of a danger to the little babes there.

Deciding that she had had enough of her house being trashed (and sharing out a child's own toys does not always work too well) she got creative. She checked out the cost of hiring the hall where the mother-and-toddler group was held. It was just £10 for an hour and they could use the toys and the kitchen. Ten mums signed up for this 'older kids group' and all donated a few toys and put some money in the kitty for refreshments and hall hire (it worked out about £1.50 each per family). The kids had their own group, mums got coffee and biscuits and no babies were at risk. Setting up your own group (but insisting everyone tidies up at the end and sets up at the start) can be a real blessing, particularly in the winter months. Don't end up out of pocket, though. Be sure everyone pays towards drinks and turns are taken doing the shopping to restock the kitchen.

So, if you can't find what you and your child really want and need locally, think about doing something yourself.

84. CUT-COST CRAFTS

Craft is a cheap and cheerful activity to do, but the prospect of glitter raining down upon your house can fill even the most dedicated crafter with dread. Kids love making things and you'll be surprised how long arts and crafts can keep them occupied and sitting still. Whether you're making gifts or customising a cereal packet, your child's dexterity and imagination will blossom while having lots of fun.

What's in the box?

I keep a big old craft box regularly stocked with the following:

Bought stuff	Cupboard stuff (bits and bobs you have at home)
Stickers, glitter, glue, feathers, plain card, colour paper, sellotape, scissors, play dough, coloured pipe cleaners, sticky foam shapes, colouring books, crayons, felt tips, paint brushes, paint, wiggly eyes, magnets to attach pictures to the fridge, shiny stars and BluTack	Lentils, curly pasta, string, toilet roll tubes, old birthday cards, buttons, beads from old bracelets, tissue from gifts, gift wrap, various old boxes, margarine tubs (for storage) and baby food jars (for paint water) old newspapers (to protect table, floor, etc) and two big old T-shirts (aprons aren't enough for my creative duo, paint has to go everywhere!)

I would say I have never wasted money on craft items as eventually they all get used and they last ages.

If you need some inspiration for your next art and craft session, here are five simple and successful projects I've done with my children.

Jungle collage

My son loves animals with such all-consuming passion that he decided he wanted to make a huge jungle picture for his bedroom. He has a fairly short concentration span when it comes to arts and crafts, so I decided we'd go for this one step at a time. We worked on one animal, a tree or a bit of sky at each session; in this way, he had lots of little craft projects to do that then built up to one fantastic picture. Our sunshine was made from dried spaghetti and yellow paint. Our trees were sticks and leaves found in the local park. Our crocodile was made from egg boxes and our flamingo from pink card and a feather from an old baby girl card. All in all we had the most brilliant and enormous picture with tons of textures and colours and we (and I mean we) were really proud. I showed everyone. Frankie has had it up in his bedroom for ages. It took weeks to make but he never got bored because we just did one thing at a time. Since then, in a similar vein, we have created our own underwater scene, and next he wants to do the North Pole.

Beautiful butterflies

Butterflies have to be some of the easiest shapes to draw. So, astound your children with various butterfly outlines (they'll think for quite a long time that you really can draw) to cut out. Then, choose whether you're going to do the classic 'butterfly painting' (where you paint on just one side of the paper and fold it over to have identical paint marks on the other side) or decorate your shape with lots and lots of shiny, spirally, glittery, tactile things to make gorgeous patterns. Two pipe cleaners stuck down the middle and curled into antennae complete the look; you can dangle a gorgeous group of butterflies on ribbons or cotton threads from the ceiling or a coat hanger.

Personalised pictures

It was the week of my birthday and my baby was just two months old and Frankie was three, and we were truly skint. That week, we felt we couldn't even go for a bag of chips, we were that poor. Naturally, I wanted a birthday present but there was no cash so I decided instead to make a very special gift with my children, for myself, that I will keep forever. We had a plain canvas knocking about and I painted Lisi's foot and Frankie's hand with acrylic paint and pressed them onto the canvas. We made the most gorgeous little snapshot of a moment in time that will always make me smile. So simple, so precious (yet so cheap) and a wonderful gift idea. It took only a matter of minutes to do.

Everyone in the family could do a footprint on a separate canvas with one foot for each member of the family and a paw print from the dog or cat. You could arrange such pictures on the wall up the stairs. Or do something similar with everyone's handprint on one canvas all going round in a circle. You could have Grandad and baby's hands side by side. You could write 'love' in multicoloured fingerprints of all sizes. Whatever you wish…it will be unique and an economical but priceless gift.

Multicoloured masterpiece

Colour a piece of card in thick stripes of crayon (all different colours). Then go over all of the stripes with black paint mixed with a little washing-up liquid. To create a multicoloured picture, just score through the black layer in whatever patterns or shape you want using a pencil or a cocktail stick. This technique works brilliantly for making firework pictures, but you can use it for pretty much anything from magical wizards and fairy-tale castles to cats and flowers – the different colours just shine through.

Sock friend

Sock puppets are as old as the hills but always fun to make and then play with. Find a coloured, no longer wanted, odd sock (I have a drawerful, in fact, where do the other halves go?). Cut out some paper circles or, if you've got some, use wiggly eyes. Glue on some wool or pipe cleaners for hair and try on for size. As you open and shut your hands you should be able to figure out where the tongue needs to go and you could sew some pink fabric in for this or glue on some red paper or felt. You will need tough glue to stick paper to fabric so it's probably best if you do that bit. Your child should be able to do the cutting (with safety scissors) and deciding on the decoration. If you make one each they can become pals (and yours can do some of your nagging for you).

All these crafts are cheap and easy to do and they will give you highly original and sure-to-be-treasured results.

I've listed some great books for craft in the Resource Bank (page 274) along with some brilliant and inspiring websites (page 273).

CHAPTER 11

Earning Money While Staying Off Work

D
o you want or need to make some money while at home with your baby, toddler or pre-schooler? As your children grow older, you're likely to be getting a good night's sleep and may even be having times without a little one at home (when they're at pre-school or round at a friend's house). So, how do you go about earning some much-need cash while still being a full-time parent? This chapter is all about making extra money and I hope that my ideas help to spark a few thoughts of your own.

85. LEGAL STUFF YOU NEED TO KNOW

First things first, everyone has the right to earn up to £5,435 each year without paying taxes. So, if your only income is from eBaying, babysitting or something similar and is no more than this allowance, you do not need to pay tax. If you exceed this amount, though, you need to let Her Majesty's Revenue & Customs know. You also need to register any new business with HMRC within three months or you may be fined.

If you are self-employed or earn money that is not taxed by an employer you may need to complete a self-assessment for tax purposes. Do call your local tax office to discuss this and to ensure you get sent a tax return if you are earning above the allotted amount (see also page 259).

If you plan to embark on a money-making venture, be aware that it could affect your eligibility for benefit payments. Inform all the relevant agencies as soon as you know about any regular income so your benefit payments can be adjusted accordingly; you do not want to end up being overpaid, owing a fortune and having all payments stopped.

Check out the government site relating to all your taxes and benefits (www.hmrc.gov.uk) and get accurate advice for earning.

One thing you may not know is that paying national insurance on a monthly basis while you're earning is essential if you later want to be able to claim maternity allowance. If you are in any doubt, consult your local tax office – they will be able to advise you fully. Contact your local tax office by searching www.hmrc.gov.uk/local/index.htm or look in your local phone book.

86. BUYING A FAMILY-FRIENDLY FRANCHISE

A popular and lucrative option among stay-at-home parents is buying a baby-related franchise. As I have said I bought a TinyTalk baby-signing franchise when my son was just nine months' old. I had rung to book Frankie and myself into our local class only to find out that the classes were all full and that the franchise was soon to be sold. I am experienced at signing, a confident singer and used to training groups and so immediately thought, 'Oh, this could be for me!' I was interviewed and approved, then trained by the company, set up with equipment and lesson plans and then you're off and running.

Running my own franchise was interesting and I earned a good income. There were over 100 mums (and one or two dads) out there running TinyTalk franchises; we would chat online or at regional and national conferences, it was a real community of support. I was able to take my son along to the classes I taught and I met lots of other local mums and their babies who have remained friends. I only worked one morning a week baby signing, yet I made enough money to keep my car on the road and pay for all my son's activities. What's more, it integrated me into our local community and I was able to contribute financially. When I sold up due to baby number two, I made a healthy profit. Plus, I got a great maternity allowance as a result of my very part-time working (this only happens if you pay your voluntary national insurance contributions, though).

During that time, I built up new skills in running a

business and these will stand me in good stead when I eventually venture back out into the workplace. Running my own baby business made me feel stimulated, proud and balanced.

There's a whole family of baby- and children-linked franchises – Tumble Tots, Jo Jingles and Socatots, to name a few – so ponder a while, it could be perfect for your current lifestyle. I worked at my franchise for three years and I loved it.

The Resource Bank lists lots of franchise ideas and contact details (page 261).

87. SELLING ON YOUR SECONDS

What could be better than selling on the things you don't need any more (decluttering as you go) for a tidy profit? And so much better (and greener) than simply throwing them out.

We covered where to shop for second-hand goods back in Chapter 2 (page 59). It's not rocket science but from my experience these are the easiest routes to exploit to make money by selling.

eBay

Everyone has a flirtation with eBay at some point in their lives but eBay can be a stay-at-home parent's best friend. You can sell almost anything and it is simple to do so. Take a photo of your item, write your listing (these can be brief) and set a starting price (and a reserve if you want to set its lowest possible price) and let it sell at auction over several days. The highest bidder gets it.

Over the years on eBay, I have sold bundles of clothes, a breast pump, toys, a steriliser, hats, maternity clothes, books, a pushchair, and so on, and I've often received a much better price than I would have imagined. For instance, I have just sold my highchair (bought for £50, sold for £25). The woman who bought it was delighted with her bargain and I can put the money towards Frankie's gymnastics classes.

Amazon

You can not only buy books at www.amazon.co.uk, you can also sell books, toys, etc., second-hand in its marketplace section. You list your item (without a photo), describe it and name a price. It sells when someone is prepared to pay that price; like eBay, amazon take a cut. It is extremely straightforward and I have sold lots of books this way, as well as a few toys.

Car boot sales

Taking part in a car boot sale can be fun and a good day out can be had by all involved. I tend to go with my mum about four times a year – without the kids and in the summer. We take chairs, a flask of coffee and sandwiches and relax and gossip while we sell from a table in front of our car. You have to cough up for your pitch (about £7–10) but after that all money you make is pure profit. Friends and family have happily given us their 'junk' to sell. At the end of the summer (and the last of our car boot opportunities), we take anything left to our local charity shop. On average, we make anything from £50 to £150 depending on the quality of your items and, of course on the weather.

Local newspapers

Most classified sections in local papers allow you to list any items for sale either free or at very low cost, so dig out that old pram, clean it up and sell it. Clothes bagged up into sizes, and long-forgotten toys all just need a good clean and a well-written pitch, and it's cash for you.

NCT nearly new sales

As already mentioned (page 61), National Childbirth Trust nearly new sales are set up to sell all goods for babies and toddlers. All items to be sold at these sales have to be of very good second-hand quality. Your local branch will have details of their sales but typically they run twice yearly. The NCT sells for you but you are expected to help out on the day and they take 25 per cent of your sale. I made good money selling on baby stuff at NCT sales.

If you are definitely planning to have more babies, you may well want to hang on to the big stuff so store it well. Things can disintegrate if left untended so don't let your Moses basket go mouldy in the shed. At the same time, don't be sentimental either: apart from keeping one or two special mementos, when you are done with an item it's time to pass it on or sell it. Funding toddler years through parting with baby stuff makes complete sense.

Netmums

It is free to sell items on the netmums website (www. netmums.com) and as you are advertising in your local area buyers will often collect, saving the hastle of packing and posting.

Check out the Resource Bank (see page 264) for details on how to find local car boots and NCT sales. Do remember to keep a tally of what you have earned.

88. ONLINE SURVEYS AND COMPETITIONS

You can earn a few pounds here and there by completing online surveys in mere minutes and, before you know it, the stash of cash will have grown. If you're online and don't mind giving out your personal information then check out www.whichsurveys.com, which lists over 200 survey companies who will pay you in cash or in prizes to take part in online surveys.

On the subject of competitions, let me tell you a story. Feeling adventurous and, to be honest, at a bit of a loose end one day when my son was two, I got him to colour in a picture from his Thomas the Tank Engine magazine and draw a link between Thomas and Percy or some such nonsense, and we went to post it off. It is the only competition I have ever entered with him and I thought nothing more of it. Six months later the most enormous box arrived out of the blue. We had won loads of new trains and various very expensive Thomas the Tank Engine items. Frankie had many of them already (we have a big, generous family) so we flogged the lot on eBay for £80 and bought our family a top day out at Thomas Land.

And that's not all. Frankie's bestest friend Jack had a photo taken with him and all his Thomas the Tank Engine trains, it got printed in a magazine and he won a lovely train book. My best friend Zelga encouraged her daughter Lilya at three years old to enter a painting competition at a local art gallery, she won and got to show off her lovely picture in the gallery window. She was so proud, and it didn't matter that there weren't any goodies on offer. So, don't write off competitions; in fact, do write off *to* competitions. My friend Catherine entered her two daughters' pictures into a drawing competition at the Early Learning Centre and bizarrely they both won. When she asked the manager about it, she said it wasn't really that much of a coincidence, since no one ever really enters kids competitions. Catherine told everyone that she knows and now, unfortunately, wins very little as a result.

Do enter competitions, someone has to win. (But don't tell too many people if it's a local competition.)

89. MARKET RESEARCH

When someone stops you on the street and asks if you read newspapers or eat a certain brand of chocolate, in the past you probably put your head down, mumbled and sped off.

Am I right? Now instead of scuttling past head bowed, I look those market researchers in the eye and have even been known to approach them instead. As a result, I have had massive boxes of free Weetabix and free orange squash. I have earned quite a few crisp tenners from talking about puzzle balls and wooden games. I have raved about the virtues of libraries to my local council as well as how I feel about Council Tax (for £50!). I have had complimentary packs of Quorn and crisps, and been given lovely snacks, glasses of wine and taxi rides in the process. Taking part in market research and focus groups can be dull, there's no denying it and is a bit time consuming, but I have had a laugh and got some great freebies along the way.

90. INFORMAL, OCCASIONAL WORK

Finding some form of informal, occasional work that fits with your lifestyle isn't always easy but some deliberation may soon throw up a few ideas. You could perhaps put a postcard in your local post office window advertising your skills, as long as they're compatible with small children. Taking in ironing is a classic example, you can easily do some in the evenings when the children are asleep or when they're watching a film on TV. Dog walking is great exercise for all (make sure it is a friendly dog, though) or if dogs aren't your thing then why not offer to look after someone's rabbit while they go on holiday? I am sure your child would love you to.

If you're more of a people person, then perhaps some kind of service is the way to go. A woman I know used to clean and shop for an older lady who had become quite frail. Her daughter would sit and play on the floor as she did a quick clean and the lady adored watching the little girl play. Perfect.

You can turn anything that fits in with your new baby- or childcentred lifestyle into a profitable little earner. Don't let such work take over, though, that's not the idea. I always try to keep my work consigned to the evening or nap or TV times as far as possible. If you think about what you are good at or skills from work that could be used flexibly at home, I am sure you can find a little job that is just right for you. Spread the word, put a free notice in your local paper and you could be in business.

For some more money-making ideas delve into the Resource Bank (page 259).

91. IS CHILDMINDING FOR YOU?

I have known quite a few mums who, keen to stay home with their children, have become registered childminders. This set-up can be ideal, as you will get to spend all day with your child and he or she will have company and so learn to share and socialise. You will also only be doing child-orientated activities. But, on the downside, your child will have to share you, their home and their toys, and not all children like this. You might find, too, that you miss the one-on-one time you have been used to with your child so perhaps start gradually or choose to look after other children only on certain days of the week.

You may fancy doing a day or two a week or you might prefer to do before and after school sessions. Or you may like the idea of the money a full-time position could earn you. Whichever you choose, you will need to register as a childminder if you provide childcare for more than two hours a day for a child who is not a blood relative. The National Childminding Association describes the benefits of childminding as having a rewarding career, being your own boss and running your own business from the comfort of your own home. They suggest your days will be varied since you can choose your own hours, plus you can care for your own kids at the same time.

Registration requires attending a briefing and a short childcare course usually run locally, attending one session a week over six weeks (see also page 259). Ofsted will inspect you and your home and you will need to have clear policies and paperwork in place in regard to your childcare practice. Support is available from the National Childminding Association as well as a start-up grant to help make any improvements to your home that may be necessary. For more specific details on how to register as a childminder and other contacts, please look in the Resource Bank (page 259).

92. FORMAL PART-TIME WORK

Another way to earn some extra cash is to have a formal part-time job that suits your family life. Can you proofread? Teach a GCSE or A-level subject privately? Take in marking for the Open University? Do regular mending for a local dry cleaner? While these sorts of jobs would probably mean working for someone else, rather than just yourself, on a more regular basis, you could still fit the work around your life by doing the work as your baby or child sleeps.

More structured, formal part-time work can range from stacking supermarket shelves during a night shift or manning reception a couple of sessions a week, to teaching an aerobics class once a week or working as a Sunday shop assistant. These part-time jobs can be easily integrated into family life (as long as your partner, extended family or friends support you) and will bring in a regular income.

Each summer I mark some university papers in the evenings and I give a lecture each February at Nottingham University. For this work I receive fixed, regular pay and, because it is regular, we can rely on this money.

I used to think that it was a real shame that our generation of women needs to bring in a second income in order to keep a home, whereas our parents (mums usually) didn't. But as I have asked around, past generations of mums have tales to tell of homeworking; sewing, typing and stuffing envelopes. Many worked night shifts or did informal but paid childminding, too. It seems full-time mums have always had to earn something to help the family get by. A regular job can give you security of income in a way dog walking just can't. Think about running a dieting class or doing bookkeeping for a small business locally. Websites such as www.workingmums. co.uk are worth checking out for home-based and part-time job opportunities.

93. CASH IN ON YOUR CRAFTY WAYS

Are you crafty? Can you bake, sew or knit? If you can, you have an amazing resource to exploit – yourself. Making something by hand can cost a fraction of its retail cost; whether it's clothes or toys for your kids, tasty cakes for tea or perhaps lovely home furnishings, any and all of the above can serve you well in the cash stakes. What's more, you'll have unique and adorable gift potential too. So, if you have a creative skill, drag it back out and dust it off as now is the time to let it shine.

If you're talented, many colleges offering night classes may well have a slot for you to teach something. If you aren't ready for a class environment, boost your confidence by taking a refresher course (usually subsidised if you are on a low income).

If you'd rather just create your own crafts, you could set yourself up to sell at craft fairs, to shops, on eBay or even on your own website. None of these areas is as complicated as it seems to break into. Our local craft fair charges just £17 a day for stalls. Find out what's coming up in the calendar and contact the organiser of any interesting and appropriate events about taking a stall. You can ask the manager in any appropriate shop if they are interested in selling your items and arrange to take some samples in for them to see. What's the worst they can say?

Selling on eBay is an area we have already explored as it is so straightforward and selling home crafts on eBay is increasingly popular. Check out www.folksy.com too as a great place to sell any home-made items. It's handy if you know someone with IT skills to help you set up your own website, then it's just a case of the right software and a couple of hundred pounds. Perhaps see how your goods sell elsewhere first before you outlay this kind of money. Ask a tech-savvy friend if they can help or perhaps find out if your local college runs courses on setting up websites. You can be a mumpreneur from your own home.

Refine your skills and practise. Most of your 'creating' can be done at home when you have a baby break (or let's be honest, more likely in the evening when the children are in bed). Look online for communities of like-minded creatives and you may well find support and inspiration.

Enjoy your creativity and make it work for you.

94. PARTIES YOU CAN PROFIT FROM

Whether you act as a host for a party or sell at parties, there is definitely profit to be made from having fun.

You may well have a friend who has bought into an enterprising scheme such as Phoenix Trading cards, Captain Tortue clothing or Usborne Books. These schemes have representatives, typically mums, selling their products directly to the consumer. Not through door knocking but at parties at people's homes or stalls at local fêtes or school fairs. Customers are often friends (or friends of friends), relatives or those from a playgroup or school. These home-based businesses fit really well into family life, as selling can be organised to suit childcare arrangements. What's more, these products sell well to other mums (hence lots of mums do it and exploit their contacts).

Alternatively, you may have a friend who sells Virgin

Vie or even the more adult-orientated Ann Summers. If you like what they are selling, do consider hosting a party at which they can sell their goods. As a host, you need to do very little except send out invites, make a few snacks and buy some soft drinks or wine. You will have lots of fun without spending any money and you will often get a bonus or a significant discount as a result of what is sold.

From my experience of hosting a children's book party (which took £250 in sales for my friend), I received almost £40 worth of books free. I turned this even more to my advantage by choosing titles to give as birthday or Christmas presents – so that was 10 presents sorted in one evening. Plus, I got to see some friends, eat lots of nibbles and not leave the comfort of my own home. Everyone had a lovely time too. So, why not get partying?

You may want to consider such a business opportunity yourself. Don't try to compete with your friends though (the market isn't that big, unless perhaps you live in London.) Find a gap in the market and invite your friends and all their contacts to host your parties. Start-up fees are generally small and you can usually work as much or as little as you like.

Check out the Resource Bank (page 263) for contact details and ideas.

95. MODELLING

Modelling could be a money-spinner for yourself or your child. You don't have to be a size zero supermodel, modelling agencies want people of all shapes and sizes.

Many moons ago when I was much, much younger I did some modelling for £15 hour. That was well over 15 years ago. I'd take that rate of pay now! Yes, it was nude (but it was for an artist recommended by an art college, honest). I'm informed by a source who wishes to remain anonymous that a life model can now earn upwards of £25 an hour. Life models come in all shapes and sizes, too, and no one is going to worry in the slightest about your frizzy hair, stretch marks and saggy tummy. Contact your local art college to see if they want a model for an hour or two a week. The money is good and they like people to look real, not airbrushed. Do be safe though and makes sure it's a reputable organisation. You'll soon get over those nerves when the money comes in, which could be a real boost.

Now, most people think their children are the most gorgeous in the world but then we are biased. If your child is a bit of a looker and it isn't only you who thinks so, it may be worth exploring the world of child modelling. You do need to live near London or another big city really because the fees aren't huge (maximum for an entire day's work is about £250, attending an audition can be just £18 and that's all before an agent's commission). Auditions are often arranged with little notice and too much travelling with a small child will just wear both of you out. The rewards can be good and the shoots can be fun and you get a professional shot of your little one to keep.

There is a great article on www.babyworld.co.uk about child modelling, which tells you what not to do and what a reputable company would ask for. In short, it suggests you don't respond to small ads in local papers that make you pay for lots of photos and probably have no modelling contacts at all and that you don't have professional photos taken at great expense. It suggests that you do check out how reputable a company is, ask to see their model book, find out how long they have been established and see how busy the company is when you go for an interview. The article also suggests doing your own research – ringing the big catalogues, such as Next or Littlewoods, and seeing which agencies they use. For a link to the babyworld article and a list of some modelling agencies look in the Resource Bank (page 262).

Local modelling competitions like 'Baby of the Year' can also be worth a go for the great prizes you can keep or sell. But do be thick-skinned and prepared for rejection. You have to accept not everyone will think little Leah is the prettiest princess of all. Of course, they are completely wrong.

96. GET PAID TO SHOP

Mystery shoppers get paid to eat out, go shopping and stay in hotels. Hands up who want to be a mystery shopper? Of course, it's not always that glamorous but it can be fun and you can earn some cash while you're out on a trip for other items anyway. Mystery shoppers are people who work undercover to test the services offered in shops to see if they're up to scratch or not. As a mystery shopper, you'd work for agencies on behalf of bigger organisations who are sussing out their own staff, competition, trends or whatever. Mystery shoppers are given their assignments, such as a meal in a restaurant, then are asked to give feedback, perhaps online, on the phone or via a questionnaire. Receipts are usually paid promptly and assignments can pay between £5 and £50.

If you fancy supplementing your shopping with some extra dosh then check out the following websites. It's free to register and who knows what exciting assignments are waiting for you?

www.grassrootsmysteryshopping.com
www.mystery-shoppers.co.uk
www.retaileyes.co.uk

CHAPTER 12

Special Occasions

Being on a budget doesn't have to mean steering clear of birthday parties or christenings. In fact, often responding to monetary constraints forces you to be creative, well organised and brave about asking for help and support, if you need it. Your baby's birthday parties can still be fun, special and memorable occasions, just resist the temptation to shell out on all sorts of unnecessary expenses. In this chapter, I pass on how I've managed to organise and survive special occasions, including Christmas, while sticking to a budget.

97. LOW-COST CHRISTENINGS AND NAMING DAYS

It won't be for everyone but some of you, for religious, spiritual, sentimental or traditional reasons (or even because of family pressure), will hold and host one of these special days for your baby. Whole books have been written on the topic, and such events can be as simple or as sophisticated as you like. Here are my ideas to mark your baby's birth in style and on a budget.

Decide what you want

Christening and naming days are all about welcoming your child to the world. Do it how you and your partner want to – this is your child. People can have very grand ideas and your parents may have friends whose granddaughter wore silk and had a marquee. But if you want to be off work with your baby, keep it simple and avoid spending big bucks on just one day. This day is not about how lavish an event you can put on, it's about family and friends, but mostly it's about your baby being welcomed your way.

Invitations

The simplest invite can be an email with perhaps a current photo attached; these are both free and environmentally friendly. If you'd prefer something tangible, then make your own invitations based on plain postcards with a little bit of pink and blue glitter writing out your baby's name with details on the back...or you could phone those on your invite list and catch up on some gossip at the same time. At least this way, you know if people are definitely coming and won't over-cater. Hand delivering wherever possible also cuts costs.

Venue

When my children were christened I hired the church hall. It cost £20 for three hours. No one had to walk far since it was next to the church, which had a car park. It was a tiny bit scruffy, but once we put out the long tables and laid out the food, decorated lots of smaller tables with plain white cloths and blew up some balloons it looked fantastic. In fact, once our loved ones filled the hall, it didn't look tatty at all.

There was plenty of room for the kids to run around too – and that can be key to a successful event, depending on the ages of the children there. We were especially lucky that there was a toy cupboard at the venue, and even luckier that a friend had the key. If your favoured venue doesn't have any toys, don't despair; just bring a selection of balls, a few trains and dolls with you (as well as the balloons)...these will keep most kids entertained for hours.

Of course, the cheapest venue is your home but whether it's a possible venue will depend on how many people are coming. If it's a summer event, it's worth taking a chance on the weather with blankets and cushions in your garden or a park near the church. Other possibilities include the homes and gardens of friends or relatives. I once asked GG, my children's wonderful Great Grandma, if she would like to host a family party for my son's birthday and she was delighted. You can still do all the work, provide refreshments and decorations, but it may just give you that bigger space you need.

Food

If you are really struggling for cash don't invite your guests at a meal time. State on the invite 'Come for coffee and cake afterwards at...' then no alcohol or feast is expected. Make such parties from 2 till 3.30pm or 10.30am till 12pm; this arrangement is perfectly acceptable and, what's more, the focus stays on the children rather than catering. The special meaning of the day is not then lost for you in a blur of preparing sandwiches and fairy cakes.

I have catered for both my children's christenings (well, I say I, but that is not strictly true.) When my mum, aunty and mother-in-law asked what we wanted as christening gifts, on both occasions we asked for help with the party food. Between the three of them they provided a buffet fit for a king and on each occasion someone bought a christening cake as a gift. They were fine about the fact that they weren't buying gifts that lasted forever because they understood how much their help meant to us.

Keep any catering simple and go for budget buys, such as quiches, carrot sticks and some little sandwiches. Nothing huge is needed or expected. I have a friend who did a huge batch of chilli and rice after her son's winter christening and it went down a treat.

Outfits

A christening or naming ceremony does demand a special outfit. But for one day, you don't want to spend a fortune on a totally impractical, white, frothy concoction that will never be worn again. I was quoted £95 for a christening dress and that was after 50 per cent had been knocked off the price. There's no need to break the bank, and after looking around I did buy something new – a gorgeous, tiny, christening dress from Next for £18. It is so beautiful that I have wrapped it in tissue to hand down to my children for their children.

Asking around within the family can reveal hidden treasures and I ended up with two wonderful, very old christening gowns (wrong size unfortunately). For my daughter's christening I was given a lovely pink shirt for my son to wear and my husband wore a similar one. My family looked smart and it cost very little. I was proud. I got a new cardi (from a supermarket for £6, but no one need know) and looked the part too. eBay sells tons of christening gowns and accessories. Remind yourself, over and over if necessary, it's an outfit for just a few hours; try not to go over the top.

Gifts

As always with gifts, if you are asked what you would like, speak up. You may need a new outfit for your baby or you may want something specific, such as a bible or a hairbrush set. If people don't ask but you know them really well and know they will be buying a gift of some kind, then you could always suggest something. Oh, and if you get a money box for your baby do look inside. We got three for Annalise's christening and only when I neglected to thank the Godparents for the cash but just mentioned the money box did they point me in the right direction. All three had money inside that I had missed.

The most important thing is to enjoy the day and show off your baby. Being thrifty won't take anything away from the magic of your day.

98. OTHER CHILDREN'S BIRTHDAYS ON A BUDGET

Other children's parties are a fantastic and free way to spend a fun afternoon with prizes, cakes and usually tears that are not your responsibility. When it comes to buying presents for your little one's friends, you really don't need to spend much, no matter how much was spent on your child or how wealthy your friends are. My answer to buying presents when you're feeling skint falls into one of three options.

- Option One: Buy exactly what you know the child will love, however small the price. A pirate sticker book, a super-fast little car, a new CD of nursery rhymes, snap cards or threading beads. All last for ages and keep the child and mum happy.
- Option Two: Go for something original – that way no one has a clue how much you have spent. Ideas can be old-fashioned (a yo-yo or a Diablo) or kitsch (think ribbon kite or a personalised T-shirt). We bought our son the coolest tops from Skegness Pier each summer with his name written on them in silver for £3. These were the most complimented piece of clothing he ever had, largely because no one else had one – they don't sell them in designer boutiques, just good old Skeggy – so they were unique!)
- Option Three: Regifting. But be careful with this one. On more than one occasion my son received the same gift twice and even at his rate of losing or breaking toys two is one too many. I couldn't return these gifts as I often had no clue where they were from. To sell them would have bought in mere

pennies and they are cracking presents so what's a girl to do? I popped them in my present box so that in future I could wrap them up and pass them on. They were brand new and the most perfect of gifts. But, and here's the but, try not to give it back to the person who gave it to your child; they (well, their mum) might be terribly upset.

99. YOUR CHILD'S BIRTHDAYS ON A BUDGET

When babies are one, birthdays tend to be small family affairs, which a baby doesn't really understand. By the time they hit two party invites start to come aplenty. At three your child fully understands birthdays and will most likely have already asked (months in advance) for a cake in the shape of…

I love my children's birthdays. When it is your child's birthday it is natural that you want to make all their dreams come true, but you'll need to do this without breaking the bank.

The present

Get them what they want if you can afford it but then absolutely nothing else. They will get a pile of presents from everyone else, just one from you is fine. If you can't afford the trampoline or sit-on car, then ask Grandma and Aunty Mo to go in with you. Have a clear idea of what your child wants or needs as others are bound to ask you. It's far better your child doesn't get jigsaws if he or she hates them and that they do get armbands if this is what they need. Be clear and precise. And, there's always the useful gift of a course of activities or clothes.

The party

A party on a shoestring sounds impossible when confronted with catalogues trying to sell you coordinated partyware, party bags and presents – as well as a bouncy castle in the garden. But it is possible, and here's how to make it so.

MAKE YOUR OWN INVITES – A sticker or two of your child's favourite character, such as a fairy, pirate or animal on a plain postcard looks so cute, is easy for your child to help with and cheap as chips. He or she will be so proud to have created invitations. Hand deliver where possible and keep the party times shortish, no more than two hours is best from my experience.

FOOD OR NO FOOD? – If you organise the party mid-afternoon you avoid the need to cater at all, and you could just write 'Please come to Frankie's party for games and cake on…' and that would really cut down your costs (and effort). If you love to put on a spread then I strongly suggest you follow the maxim that less is more: simple little sandwiches, a few crisps, slices of apples, raisins and cheeses slices would be fine. Don't go mad with cakes and chocolate biccies as not everyone is happy about later collecting a child that's totally wired, but do get some treats, otherwise it wouldn't be a party, would it? Ask parents when they arrive about any food allergies, and tell parents to help themselves and their own children to food so you don't make a mistake. It's a good idea to keep all packaging in case anyone needs to check ingredients.

CONSIDER A THEME – Themes are fun but can be expensive. One year my little boy was really into Thomas the Tank Engine and I foolishly ended up buying Thomas cups, tablecloth and napkins all to be used once then thrown away. So, rather than buying a raft of coordinated party plates and bags etc, ask all the guests to come in fancy dress (encourage home-made outfits so no one spends too much) or make it a beach party with the sandpit out and a crafty activity to make some funky sunglasses out of card. Fancy dress spreads the effort and can make for lots of giggles even with the littlest kids. As for cardboard plates and cups forget it…a cheap plastic set from Ikea can last you a party lifetime.

Low cost Hallowe'en – I held a Hallowe'en party recently just for three little kids. They all dressed up and we 'trick or treated' two of my friends and my mum. Then, we had races with plastic spiders and cut out bats, and just cheered the winner. We coloured in spider pictures, I read a spider story and we sang 'Little Miss Muffet' and 'Incy Wincy Spider'. We had a brilliant time. For the food, I got a few snacks out my cupboard. The whole event cost me £2.99 for Frankie's monster mask, which being a mask not a costume will fit for years. Top party, no tears, lots of fun and little cost. It can be done and to be honest anything that stops our children thinking it's all about receiving is a good thing.

PRIZE-FREE GAMES – Do away with prizes. Now, that might sound mean but how many tiny toys gathered from parties ever actually get played with? They're greeted with an excited look then discarded as quickly. I see them as an unnecessary expense and cause of upset at almost every party. I find that prizes bring out greediness in children too unsophisticated to hide their disappointment. They can also cost a packet. I tried to do cheap pass-the-parcel gifts once, only to have them looked at with derision by two-year-olds and most were left behind at the end of the party. These little crayon packs and bouncy balls had cost about £5 – what a complete waste.

My favourite party games

I have a cousin who works at a Steiner school (creative, natural and anti-plastic) and she taught me a variation on pass-the-parcel that I always use now, and it works a treat with little kids.

Sing-along pass-the-parcel – After each layer of paper rather than a chocolate or a little gift you have a piece of paper with a song title and the group (that's parents too) have to sing the song. Action songs work particularly well and the kiddies love it. You do need to make sure you know the words though and sing up. Alternatively, have little challenges written on the paper, such as spin round three times, jump on one foot for one minute or shake your neighbours hand; nothing too hard, just simple and fun.

Hunt the birthday cake – Hide cut-out pictures of cake around the garden (or inside works well too) and send everyone off to find one picture. The prize? They swap the picture for a slice of birthday cake.

Diddy disco – Get some music on and get on down at the disco.

Penalty shoot out – If there has to be a winner, a big clap and a cheer (or if you're feeling ambitious a Mexican wave) is good enough.

Party bags

Please don't go down the party bag route – it's expensive and feeds into a consumeristic culture. Instead, give the children a slice of cake and maybe a balloon, say thanks and bye-bye. I have often found unexplored party bags in my car weeks after a party.

Birthday cake

If someone you know can bake and will make you a cake as a gift then rope them in straight away. Or make your own. Professionally made cakes can steal precious pounds from your party budget. Is it really worth a big expense? If you can't face making it yourself and can't find a friend to bake, hit the supermarket and ask if Grandpa would like to pay for it as a gift. These cakes are usually reasonably priced and large and, if you want to satisfy your little one's penchant for Mr Men or Spiderman, then supermarkets will usually have something to fit the bill.

I could go on and on about parties; I love them. Essentially they're supposed to be fun, don't stress and don't end up spending all the time in the kitchen or your child's special day gets lost. Lighten up and smile, they always work out, and really don't need to cost too much.

100. AN INEXPENSIVE, STUPENDOUS CHRISTMAS

I have to mention Christmas because it is the one time of year mums and dads on a budget can truly dread. Presents for everyone, sumptuous meals, party clothes and a tree to buy and decorate, can just be too much.

So, follow my top 10 tips for a stress-free Christmas without breaking the bank.

1. Get an artificial tree

It doesn't have to be forever, but for the next few years at least an artificial tree makes total money sense. As long as it sparkles kids are usually happy. Plus, you will be doing your bit for the environment. My Aunty Jane spray paints a big twig in gold and hangs baubles off that. It doesn't take up much room, looks gorgeous and costs almost nothing. When your babies are small or your toddlers are liable to knock over a tree, such a focus can still feel Christmassy.

2. Let someone else cook Christmas dinner

Invite yourself over to relatives for Christmas day, which will save you time, money and stress. You can have a lovely time at home over the rest of the Christmas break having done your family and/or friends proud with a Christmas day visit. You will also have saved a fortune on the way. Your family will love to see you, you house will still be tidy when you return and you can leave when you like. It makes perfect sense.

3. Try to buy your child just one small gift

Your baby or child is bound to get an enormous pile of presents from everyone else, so stick with one gift from you. It's much better that you have regular time with your kids than you spend all year working extra to pay off Christmas.

4. Buy a Christmas outfit

Get one or two nice combinations of clothes that are classy and classic, then they'll easily see you through the next few years. Change your earrings, hair and make up and no one will ever know. Black is always a winner.

5. Make your Christmas special with traditions, not things

Traditions last forever in a family, unlike the plastic ride-on toy that set you back £50. In our house, we light a candle and tell the Christmas story all cuddled up together on Christmas Eve. We go to the nativity at our local church on Christmas Eve too. We walk round the park after breakfast on Christmas Day. My husband and I write little poems that describe where we have hidden tiny gifts around the house on Boxing Day. We wrap up three old (but good) toys and take them to a homeless shelter. Each family will have its own traditions, but now is the time to make up your own and stop the all-consuming materialism. Try and make Christmas about families, friends and togetherness not about how much money you can spend.

6. Be thrifty

Transform last year's Christmas cards into tags for this year's presents; your child is sure to enjoy threading ribbon through the holes and practising their cutting skills (or you can do it in front of the TV one night). Always reuse gift bags (they cost a bomb) and salvage nice wrapping paper throughout the year, if you can. Regift where appropriate and remember, if you see a bargain during the year, scoop it up and put it to one side for Christmas. Have a present drawer or box so you know where you have put them.

7. Make gifts

If you're a whizz in the kitchen then put these talents to good use. Why not make some lovely shortbread and present it in a clear bag with a festive red ribbon? Or cook up a lovely pot of seasonal jam or chutney. If you're more crafty than cheffy, there may be a baby needing a handknitted blanket or a much-loved pet needing a portrait. Home-made presents are much more appreciated, so if you can, do take the time to make some. Write a beautiful poem and have it framed, or have a photo shoot with your kids and frame a great shot for doting grandparents. For a present that lasts all year, plant some bulbs in a sweet little pot or take some cuttings from your garden and present them in a little row of pots. Garden pots can be bought cheaply from garden centres and you can personalise them or decorate them easily. It is possible to give valuable gifts that haven't cost you much in the way of money but ooze thought and care. The things we treasure most often cost the least.

8. Don't try to keep up

You are not going to be able to afford the same kinds of presents as your bank manager sister who works full-time and has no kids, so don't even try. You are not at the same place in your life right now. She would probably love a gorgeous photo of her nephews and nieces just as much as you would enjoy the designer handbag she buys you (well, nearly as much).

9. Have a present amnesty

Once someone buys a gift for your child, you are inextricably involved in a circle of gifting, and you will need to return the favour. To keep your present buying to the minimum, talk to your close friends in advance (say, November) and say that rather than do Christmas gifts you think it would be much better to stick to just birthdays as the children get so much. They will probably be mightily relieved.

10. Club together for bigger gifts

I have a friend who lives in Mold in Wales and it is quite usual there that gifts of money are given on a child's birthday and used by the parents to buy a bigger gift for the child. You can follow their lead if you want to get something substantial at Christmas and no single person would be able to afford it. By grouping together, our family managed to buy three-year-old Frankie his Thomas the Tank Engine bed. Ask those close to you for contributions towards something bigger if that's going to be best for you and your child.

Whatever you do for Christmas, here are three very important don'ts.

- Don't splurge madly and think, 'Oh it's Christmas, I just have to buy this, that and the other.' It might take you all year to pay off, and it really isn't necessary to spend to have a good time.
- Don't stress. Whatever you believe in, Christmas is meant to be a wonderful family time. Relax, keep calm and you will have a magical time without all the paraphernalia. As long as you are enthusiastic, happy and content your family Christmas will be good enough.

- Don't feel guilty about what you can't afford to do or buy. Look back on a year of togetherness and be proud of what you achieved.

Have a very happy Christmas.

101. HOW TO AFFORD...BABY NUMBER TWO

I really wanted and was lucky enough to have another baby, though I realise not everyone wants more than one child. We deliberated about whether we could afford baby number two for quite a while until I realised that I was looking at it only from the extra cost side of things rather than trying to see the positives:

- you get additional child benefit, and an increase in your allowances
- you will already have most of the equipment you need (if you can find the damn screws for the cot and the stair gates)
- you save money as your children will eventually entertain each other
- your experiences as a mother may mean that baby number two may bring you twice the joy and half the stress

My only extra expense in the first year was a few pink clothes and the usual nappies and toiletries.

Don't put off having a baby because of money, you will never ever look back and think that was a smart decision.

If you and your partner want another child and can, then you should. You will manage. As my mum points out people used to have six or seven on a regular basis and they didn't stress half as much as I did with one, and they probably had far less money.

Conclusion

You will learn so much along your parenting path, hopefully from books like this and from your own experiences. You will learn a lot too from contacts you meet along the way. All babies benefit from time at home with their parents, so do help others by sharing your money-savvy knowledge. You could post any tips and ideas that worked for you on websites like www.netmums.co.uk or perhaps you could write a blog. Maybe you could send your top cost-saving tips into a parenting magazine or your local newspaper and get paid for them. Even if you just talk to all the parents you meet and endeavour to share one good idea with each (such as where that brilliant second-hand baby clothes shop is or where you got your pram serviced really cheaply), you will do two marvellous things:

1. You will help build a community of mums who help each other out and do away with this competitive element that comes creeping in. Maybe we can then show each other how to breastfeed, wean, relieve colic and cope without the need to pay a stranger to help us out.

2. You might just help another parent realise they can cope with less money and consequently reduce their hours at work to spend more time with their baby, or even just take their full maternity entitlement. You know that's a good thing and everyone's a winner.

Do be a goodwill ambassador for baby budgeting.

P.S. Do check out www.babybudgeting.co.uk for a regularly updated baby budgeting blog and to see and share money saving tips.

I wish you many happy baby days.

The Resource Bank

To save you time and energy locating useful information, I've grouped together helpful websites, books, phone numbers and information that you may need in your quest to afford time off with your baby. By using this Resource Bank you'll be able to enjoy a coffee in the sunshine, walk to feed the ducks or even have an early night instead of trawling for this information yourself. I hope you find everything you need to get started here. This is not a definitive list, by any means, but it is a varied selection of useful, quality information that I have used successfully or has been tried or tested by someone I know.

Of course, lots of other great classes, websites and books do exist and you will definitely come across some brilliant stuff locally too. If you do, that is fantastic. Tell your friends and spread the word; there's a blank section right at the back for you to note down and add constantly to personalise your resource bank. Keeping all your information together will save you a lot of time in locating scraps of paper and missing leaflets.

For quick reference, we've grouped the information into the following topics:

Getting Information or Support

If you are pregnant or have just had a baby, remember that you should speak to your midwife, GP or health visitor if you have any worries.

BABY ACTIVITIES

There are many, many more baby activity organisations and sites than I have listed – that would take a hefty book in its own right. I have listed the biggest organisations, the most highly recommended to me and, where possible, those I have experienced myself. I am sure you will find many more.

If you're new to an area or haven't heard what's on locally, then you can find out what's on by using one of the following directories.

All 4 kids

All 4 Kids is a comprehensive directory website and a quick and easy way to find everything from school uniforms and children's toys to designer clothes and family skiing holidays. What's more, it has a full list of children's activity classes (it is particularly strong on those in the London area).
www.all4kidsuk.com

Baby discos

Enjoy some time 'to get on down' with your little one at a specially organised event.

Baby Loves Disco
Based in London and Manchester, at these events you'll find real DJs playing real music, bubble machines, egg shakers, dance

scarves, chill out area, face painting, nappy changing stations, a full spread of healthy snacks, juice boxes and lots of dancing.
07748 321266
www.babylovesdisco.co.uk
elaine@babylovesdisco.co.uk

Boogie Babies

Based in Nottingham and Derby, this company offers tons of fun in a cool nightclub – something for the whole family.
www.boogie.moonfruit.com

Disco Loco

This London-based dance-floor mash-up is for the whole family. Adults can join the kids hula-hooping and dancing to music from Al Green to The Cure, or relax in the lounge with coffee and cake. Children (tots to tweenies) can email music requests in advance for the event, which takes place every month on a Sunday afternoon in Hackney.
info@chatspalace.com

Baby massage

Baby massage is a great bonding experience for babies and their carers, and one that both participants may well find deeply relaxing, both emotionally and physically. Classes are a lovely way to meet local babies but baby massage can also be self-taught and practised at home.

This book is a fantastic read and manual for finding out more on the subject and learning techniques: Vimala McClure, *Infant Massage – A handbook for loving parents* (Souvenir Press, 2001).

Contact the International Association of Infant Massage, which offers comprehensive training before certifying their instructors, and they will direct you to your nearest certified massage instructor.
020 8989 9597
www.iaim.org.uk

Information on massage cited within this book (see page 114) is from Tracey Winston CIMI who runs baby massage courses based in Nottinghamshire. Contact her on Traceywinston2003@yahoo.com for further information.

Baby music

There's probably a different company offering a class on every day of the week, so you'll be sure to find one that suits you and your baby.

Caterpillar Music

These sessions provide an introduction to music in a fun atmosphere and are full of lively songs. There are different weekly themes and the leaders use lots of great puppets. The first class is free so you get to 'try before you buy'.

0870 199 90 90
www.caterpillarmusic.com
havefun@caterpillarmusic.com

Jo Jingles

These fun music and singing classes have an educational slant for babies and children aged from six months to five years. Jo Jingles classes aim to enhance a child's pre-school education by stimulating their interest and enjoyment of music using a series of varied and fun-themed musical programmes. Many of my friends have been to these classes and without exception have loved them.

01494 778989
www.jojingles.com

Monkey Music

Weekly sessions take place during school term time and are led by specially trained Monkey Music teachers. Throughout a 30-minute class the teachers engage the attention of both children and carers alike using catchy music, percussion instruments, colourful visual props – and boundless energy! Classes run throughout the UK.

01582 766464

www.monkeymusic.com

info@monkeymusic.com

Baby signing

Tiny Talk run baby signing classes which teach pre-verbal babies to communicate through sign. Classes involve singing, signing and socialising. TinyTalk has a great website with a handy map to find your local class, an interactive bulletin board to share signing chat and loads of articles to explain the benefits of signing. Tinytalk teach only BSL signs to babies in their classes so babies learn a skill for life.

01483 301444

www.tinytalk.co.uk

Baby swimming

Your local leisure centre or swimming pool can probably point you in the direction of a variety of baby swimming classes.

I never went to Waterbabies classes myself but I have heard only wonderful things about them. Waterbabies is the UK's largest national baby swimming company and teaches courses of baby swimming to under-fives. Just type in your postcode to find classes near you.

www.waterbabies.co.uk

Baby yoga

For baby yoga classes near you, ask your health visitor or at your local health centre.

Baby Yoga DVD

This DVD shows you how to engage your baby 0–18 months in yoga exercises. There is also a toddler version available for those from 10 months. Both are medically approved DVDs presented by an experienced teacher, Francine Freedman.

020 7289 1439

www.thebabyyogacompany.com

questions@thebabyyogacompany.com

YogaBugs

YogaBugs is a complete form of yoga exercise for children aged two-and-a-half to seven. It is a particularly good way for children to exercise on rainy days, and it benefits both their minds, through focusing on the breathing and visualisation techniques, and their bodies, through the posture work. YogaBugs is the only national franchise of children's yoga classes I have come across but it only starts from two-and-a-half.

020 8772 1800

www.yogabugs.com

info@yogabugs.com

Busy Little Ones

This online activity directory can find you all the great baby and toddler activities near you. You can search by class type or you can do a general search by area. Membership is free. You can also find class reviews and chat rooms.

www.busylittleones.co.uk

The Baby Sensory Experience

Baby Sensory classes provide hundreds of simple activities that are fun for babies from birth to 13 months. Their classes include activities ranging from signing and fibre-optic light shows to amazing light balls and bubbles and bells. They are particularly suitable for newborn babies and babies with special needs and/or a disability. There are dads-only classes too.

01344 412072 or 01722 320779

www.babysensory.co.uk

info@babysensory.co.uk

What's on 4 Little Ones?

This website has comprehensive details of the classes and activities in your area for under-fives. It's also completely free to search. All the information is quickly available, dates, times and everything else you need to know, including links to websites and contact information plus a map to get you there. Find parent and toddler groups, gymnastics, swimming classes, dance classes, messy play, baby signing classes, pre-school and playgroups and much more all local to you.

www.whatson4littleones.co.uk

BABYSITTING CIRCLES

The following websites give examples of various ways to set up baby-sitting circles, details of schemes local to you and more general information around babysitters. Some even offer opportunities to set up your scheme online.

www.babysitclub.co.uk/parentcircles.html

www.kidsguide.co.uk/baby_and_pre-school/baby_sitting_circle.html

www.thebabybank.com

Be safe! When leaving your baby with anyone it is always advisable to go on personal recommendations and/or ask for references. The NSPCC recommends that a babysitter should be at least 16 years old.

BENEFITS

For all online advice regarding benefit entitlements, visit www.direct.gov.uk

Child and Working Tax Credits

Tax Credits Helpline on 0845 300 3900.

Child Benefit

Child Benefit Office on 08453 021 444 (open 8am–8pm, Monday to Sunday).
www.hmrc.gov.uk/childbenefit/index.htm

Maternity Allowance

Job Centre Plus on 0800 055 6688 (open 8am–6pm, Monday to Friday).
www.jobcentreplus.gov.uk

BREAST- AND BOTTLE-FEEDING SUPPORT

One of the most common concerns among new mothers is feeding their babies. All of the agencies below can help you if you have any questions or worries.

Annabel Karmel – bottle feeding

Annabel is an expert on baby food and nutrition. If you go to her site and click on the pregnancy and newborn icon you're taken to a page with many different options. There's a comprehensive section on the ins and outs of bottle-feeding.
www.annabelkarmel.com

You will also find almost all the major formula brands have their own websites with bottle-feeding advice. Look on your formula label for the correct link or telephone helpline.

La Leche League

La Leche League offers advice and information on breastfeeding, local groups and counsellors. They often hold local meetings, which you can attend to meet other nursing mothers and will often have outside speakers, too.
0845 120 2918 (open 24 hours a day)
www.laleche.org.uk
enquiries@laleche.org.uk

The Association of Breastfeeding Mothers

All telephone breastfeeding counsellors are volunteers who have breastfed their own children and have also received in-depth training on all aspects of breastfeeding.

08444 122 949 breastfeeding helpline (open 9.30am–10.30pm every day)

www.abm.me.uk

counselling@abm.me.uk

The Breastfeeding Network

The system will automatically connect you to your local breastfeeding supporter by recognising the area you are calling from, anywhere in the UK.

National Breastfeeding Helpline 0300 100 0212 (open 9.30am–9.30pm every day)

www.breastfeedingnetwork.org.uk

The National Childbirth Trust

This organisation gives advice and guidance on breastfeeding, weaning and all aspects of pregnancy and childcare. They will be able to provide local support for you.

0300 33 00 770 (Enquiries)

0300 33 00 771 (Breastfeeding)

0300 33 00 772 (Pregnancy and birth)

www.nctpregnancyandbabycare.com

CAMPING AND CARAVANNING INFORMATION – CAMPING GUIDES

Eurocamp

Eurocamp offer camping and self-catering holidays on superbly equipped holiday parks throughout Europe and the USA with a choice of accommodation, such as tents, mobile homes or chalets at bargain prices.

0844 406 0402

www.eurocamp.co.uk

The Camping and Caravanning Club

This club exists to help campers and caravanners make the most of their hobby by providing over 4,000 places to camp across the UK and worldwide.

0845 130 7632

www.campingandcaravanningclub.co.uk

UK Campsite

This useful and comprehensive website details caravan sites and camping sites in the UK.

www.ukcampsite.co.uk

See also www.coolcamping.co.uk for ideas for camping in the UK and in Europe and this useful book: Jonathan Knight, Paul Marsden and Andy Stothert, *Cool Camping England, 2nd edn* (London, Punk Publishing, 2008).

DEBT COUNSELLING AND SUPPORT

There are a host of helpful websites and free helplines if you find yourself in a difficult financial situation.

Citizens Advice Bureau

The Citizens Advice Bureau service helps people resolve their legal, financial and other problems by providing free information and advice from over 3,000 locations. Advice is available face-to-face and by telephone. Most bureaux offer home visits and some also provide email advice.

020 7833 2181

www.citizensadvice.org.uk

For practical, reliable, up-to-date information including FAQs in English, Welsh, Bengali, Gujarati, Punjabi, Urdu and Chinese on a wide range of topics (from housing and family to discrimination and benefits) and downloadable factsheets visit www.adviceguide.org.uk.

Consumer Credit Counselling Service

CCCS is a charity dedicated to providing confidential, free counselling and money management assistance to financially distressed families and individuals.

0800 138 1111 (open 8am–8pm, Monday to Friday)

www.cccs.co.uk

National Debtline

This organisation offers expert advice on the full range of debts from rent arrears to congestion charges. They deal with telephone, email and written enquiries, and can also assist callers with setting up debt-management plans.

0808 808 4000 (open 9am–9pm Monday to Friday; 9.30am–1pm Saturday)

www.nationaldebtline.co.uk

Payplan

Payplan is the UK's largest provider of free debt solutions, including free debt management plans. They will deal with your creditors on your behalf.

0800 716 239

www.payplan.com

ENVIRONMENTAL ISSUES

Change The World For A Fiver (London, We Are What We Do, 2004).

This beautiful and fabulous book is packed with ideas for children and adults alike. It's published by We Are What We Do, a social change movement whose aim is to inspire people to use their everyday actions to change the world.

020 7396 7463

www.wearewhatwedo.org

FEEDING

Cookbooks for the first few years

Kate Colquhoun, *The Thrifty Cookbook: 476 ways to eat well with leftovers* (London, Bloomsbury, 2009).

Rose Elliot and Juliet Gellatley, *Vegetarian and Vegan Mother and Baby Guide* (Bristol, Viva!, 2008).

Gina Ford, *The Gina Ford Baby & Toddler Cook Book* (London, Vermilion, 2005).

Gina Ford, *The Contented Little Baby Book Of Weaning* (London, Vermilion, 2006).

Annabel Karmel, *New Complete Baby and Toddler Meal Planner* (London, Ebury Press, 2008).

Annabel Karmel, *Top 100 Baby Purees: 100 Quick and easy meals for a healthy and happy baby* (London, Ebury Press, 2005).

Pamela Le Bailly, *Second Time Around: Ideas and recipes for leftovers* (Oxford, Trafford Publishing, 2007).

Sara Lewis, *Practical Parenting Weaning* (London, Pyramid Paperbacks, 2008).

Rosie Sykes, Polly Russell and Zoe Heron, *The Kitchen Revolution: Change the way you cook and eat forever – and save time, effort, money and food* (London, Ebury, 2008).

Carol Timperley and Stephen May, *Baby and Child Vegetarian Recipes: Over 150 healthy and delicious dishes for your young family* (London, Ebury Press, 1997).

GIFT LISTS

Gift lists enable you to set up a wish list of nursery, baby and toddler products. Such lists benefit the parents as well as the gift-giver, ensuring that the parents do not receive duplicate gifts and that the gift-giver purchases a truly valued present. Increasingly more stores offer this service.

Argos

This service allows you to register and manage your list online, lets your friends and family shop and orders your gifts for home delivery, 24 hours a day, seven days a week.

www.argos.co.uk

(Scroll to the bottom of the page and look under Argos services to find the link to Gift List link.)

John Lewis Baby Gift List

Visit your local branch to set a list up; once it's up and running you can access it online and by phone.

www.johnlewisgiftlist.com

Mamas & Papas

0845 268 2000

www.mamasandpapas.co.uk/stores/baby_gift_list.php

Mothercare

Go to your nearest store or checkout their website.

www.mothercare.com

What I'd Love

At this website you can build your own gift list from any variety of shops, which stops you being limited to just one retailer.

www.whatidlove.co.uk

LIBRARIES

To find all the branches, along with opening times, of your local library network, call your local council or check out the details on their website. Your copy of the yellow pages will also point you in the right direction.

NAPPIES

Real versus disposable? Unbleached or biodegradable? Wash yourself or nappy service? So many questions surround our decisions on nappies. Fortunately, there's a host of really informative services to help you.

The Nappy Information Service

This site focuses on the benefits of disposable nappies and gives another perspective on the great nappy debate. There is also the opportunity to put questions to a panel of experts.
www.nappyinformationservice.co.uk

The Nappy Lady

This website is great for those starting out with cloth or real nappies as it has a free, tailored advice service that takes some details from you then guides you in the right direction. You can also buy nappies at a discount on this site.
0845 652 6532
www.thenappylady.co.uk

The Real Nappy Campaign

This great site answers lots of questions about real nappies and directs you to an incentive scheme near you. You just type in your postcode.
0845 850 0606
www.realnappycampaign.com

The Used Nappy Company

At this auction site you can buy and sell real (clean!) used nappies. There's no listing fee, no photo fees – sellers pay just 5 per cent of the final sale price to the website. Over 1,000 nappy transactions are completed each month on this site.
www.usednappies.co.uk

NEWS UPDATES

First, it's good to be able to catch the headlines at a glance in a snatched moment. Here are my stalwarts for news.

www.bbc.co.uk

www.timesonline.co.uk
www.uk.reuters.com

And it's always good to indulge the ridiculous and superficial sides of life too.

www.femalefirst.co.uk/celebrity
www.handbag.com/celebrity-gossip
www.thedailygoss.com

ONLINE PARENTING COMMUNITIES

Here are a selection of online baby sites where communities of mums meet and share their tips and advice.

www.netmums.com
Netmums is a unique local network for mums with a wealth of information and advice on being a mum or indeed dad in your home town.

Other sites that offer forums to discuss issues or concerns with other parents, advice and baby related articles, include:

www.askbaby.com
www.babycentre.co.uk
www.babyworld.co.uk
www.bounty.com/newarrivals
www.thebabywebsite.com
www.ukparentslounge.com

POSTNATAL FITNESS

Before you start on regaining your pre-pregnancy body, read this sensible article covering a wide range of issues relating to postnatal exercise. (It also states very clearly: Always check with your GP or midwife before starting any new exercise or eating regime.)
www.babyworld.co.uk/information/newparents/post_baby_shape-up.asp

Ever more classes targeted specifically at new mums with little babes are springing up all over the country so you should be able to find one near you. Contact your local sports centre to find a class or log onto www.postnatalexercise.co.uk. All instructors listed on this site are fully trained to work with new mothers.

Mummies and Buggies

An hourly session of this postnatal fitness class contains a low-impact aerobics routine to help mums regain their pre-pregnancy fitness levels, toning and strengthening exercises to re-align posture and strengthen muscles, and stretching/relaxation exercises to lengthen tight muscles and relieve tension. Classes are set to launch nationally.

Claire Mockridge

07747 656550

www.mummiesandbuggies.co.uk

claire@mummiesandbuggies.co.uk

Powerpramming

If you want to get fit and know that baby is safe and happy you could give Powerpramming™ a go. This postnatal exercise group with buggies helps women all over South London get back their pre-pregnancy shape while meeting other mums.

www.powerpramming.co.uk

Pushy Mothers

Pushy Mothers is a buggy-based workout that usually takes place in parks (pretty much nationwide) and provides a safe place for mums to exercise with their babies and get together.

www.pushymothers.com

PRE-SCHOOL AND PLAYGROUPS

Depending on where you live, it might be easy to find out from walking around where the pre-schools and playgroups are locally. But for a more comprehensive look at these early years' services, check out any of the following.

ChildcareLink

This government service provides information and advice on all aspects of childcare.
0800 234 6346
www.childcarelink.gov.uk

Early Years

028 9066 2825
www.early-years.org

Scottish Pre-school Play Association

0141 221 4148
www.sppa.org.uk

The Pre-school Learning Alliance

020 7697 2500
www.pre-school.org.uk

Wales Pre-school Playgroups Association

029 2045 1242
www.walesppa.org
info@walesppa.org

You can get the telephone number of your nearest Children's Information Service (who will advise you on all children's services in your area) by calling 0800 234 6346.

TOILETRIES

Dr Stephen Antczak and Gina Antczak, *Cosmetics Unmasked: Your family guide to safe cosmetics and allergy-free toiletries* (London, Thorsons, 2001).

This book has a really great section on baby products – what we really don't need and what we should look out for. It has simple, clear advice and can stop you spending money on products that may even be harmful.

TOY LIBRARIES

The National Association of Toy and Leisure Libraries maintains a comprehensive list of toy and leisure libraries operating in the UK.
020 7428 2288
www.natll.org.uk

WALKING RESOURCES

Get out in the fresh air, whether it's an afternoon out or a weekend walking, make the most of our country's beautiful landscapes and introduce your children to the wonders of walking.

Walking holidays

A cheap and fun walking holiday can always be had at a youth hostel (which sometimes have very lovely family rooms, too). Some are basic, some are luxurious but all are affordable. You will find them countrywide.

Youth Hostels Association England & Wales
01629 592700
www.yha.org.uk

Youth Hostels Association in Scotland
01786 891400
www.syha.org.uk

For a comprehensive list of family walk books check out:
www.ramblers.org.uk/info/everyone/familywalks.html
or ask at your local bookshop for any books on family walks in your local area.

Walks with children

Check out the Ramblers Association for great tips on walking with your children:
www.ramblers.org.uk/info/everyone/children.html

There is a comprehensive *Walks with Children* series with 20 shorter walks in each, starting from playgrounds or recreation areas with observation games and recommended refreshment breaks along the way. All books are £6.95.

Making Money

If you're considering or have even started to work for yourself, you'll need to register as self-employed or as a new employee. The following places should offer all the information you're likely to need:

www.hmrc.gov.uk
www.workingforyourself.co.uk
The Self-Assessment Helpline is 0845 9000 404 (open 8am–8pm, seven days a week).
The Self-Employed Helpline is 0845 915 4655 (open 8am–5pm, Monday to Friday).

CHILDMINDING

If you're thinking of becoming a childminder, there are six specific steps to registration:

1. Attend a pre registration briefing session arranged by local authority or NCMA. Call ChildcareLink (see overleaf) for details.
2. Read all the information you are given at the session about national standards for childminding as you will have to show your Ofsted inspector you can meet these requirements.
3. Complete and return an Ofsted application pack. Ofsted will then send you information on how to apply for a CRB check (criminal records bureau) for everyone in your home over 16 years of age.

4. Ofsted will contact you to arrange for a home inspection. They will check your home is child friendly and you are suitable to care for children.
5. Take an introductory course in childminding and first aid.
6. Pay your Ofsted registration fee, receive your certificate and you are good to go.

(The above information is based on 'Become a Registered Childminder', available as a download from the NCMA, see below.)

The following organisations also offer help and advice about childminding:

ChildcareLink

Childcare Link can give you details of your local early years' teams and children's information service, both of which can help you as you start your childminding career.
0800 096 0296
www.childcarelink.gov.uk

National Childminding Association

The NCMA is the professional association for registered childminders and offers help and advice on a wide range of issues related to home-based childcare.
0800 169 4486
www.ncma.org.uk

Ofsted

Ofsted is the national government body that registers and inspects childminders.
0845 601 4771 (open 8am–8pm)
Family information service 0800 234 6346
www.ofsted.gov.uk
enquiries@ofsted.gov.uk

FRANCHISES

If you want to earn money in a way that fits with being a full-time parent then buying and running a franchise could work for you. Most websites have contact details where you can express an interest in the franchise, along with FAQs.

Jo Jingles

Music classes for babies and pre-schoolers.
01494 778989
www.jojingles.com

Monkey Music

Music and percussion classes for under-fives.
01582 766464
www.monkeymusic.com

Musical Minis

Fun music group for babies and toddlers.
020 8868 0001
www.musicalminis.co.uk

Socatots

Football coaching programme for under-fives.
0113 244 2005
www.socatots.com

TinyTalk

Baby signing classes.
01483 301444
www.tinytalk.co.uk

Tumble Tots

Baby and toddler gymnastics.
0121 585 7003
www.tumbletots.com

Yogabugs

Fun, creative yoga classes for kids aged two to seven.
www.yogabugs.com

For all the information you could possibly want about franchises on one site with lots of tips, ideas and franchise opportunities, check out www.whichfranchise.com.

GENERAL ADVICE

Money Magpie

This website has a wealth of ideas from selling your video recordings to YouTube to recycling, making money from old mobiles and Avon. Click the 'making money' tab for inspiration.
www.moneymagpie.com or buy the book *The Money Magpie*

Mum and Working

This website has extensive information on franchise opportunities, articles on setting up your own business and profiles of mums with part-time jobs. It is packed full of brilliant ideas for full-time mums to earn a bit of extra cash.
www.mumandworking.co.uk

MODELLING

Before your enrol your child or yourself with a model agency, read this useful article:
www.babyworld.co.uk/information/newparents/baby_modelling.asp

Elisabeth Smith

0845 872 1331
www.elisabethsmith.co.uk
models@elisabethsmith.co.uk

Norrie Carr Agency

020 7525 1771

www.norriecarr.com

info@norriecarr.com

Scallywags

020 8553 9999

www.scallywags.co.uk

info@scallywags.co.uk

MYSTERY SHOPPING

If you fancy earning some extra readies in the retail sector, then check these out.

Grass Roots

www.grassrootsmysteryshopping.com

Mystery Shoppers

01409 255025

www.mystery-shoppers.co.uk

sales@mystery-shoppers.co.uk

Retail Eyes

01908 328000

www.retaileyes.co.uk

support@retaileyes.co.uk

PARTY AGENTS

Becoming a party agent is an easy earning opportunity to fit into your full-time life as a mum.

Captain Tortue Clothes

Selling designer clothes (kids and women's) in houses to other mums (an easy group for you to find).
01403 754040
www.captaintortue.com

Phoenix Trading

Selling cards, tags, gift-wrap and accessories through fairs, stalls, house parties, etc.
www.phoenix-trading.co.uk

Stardust Kids

Selling designer children's clothes at house parties and coffee mornings to other mums.
020 8678 1018
www.stardustkids.co.uk

Usborne Books

Selling books for young children at house parties and events, usually to other mums.
01865 883731
www.usbornebooksathome.co.uk

SELLING YOUR SECONDS AND FINDING BARGAINS

Throughout the book I tell you which items to sell, which to lend and where to find those bargains. Here's a list of all those places in one handy location.

Car boot sales

To find details of local car boots, go to www.carbootjunction.com.

eBay

Buy and sell at an online auction at www.ebay.co.uk.

Freecycle

Whether you've decluttered and want to pass on items or are looking for free baby equipment, check out www.freecycle.org in your area.

NCT nearly new sales

Kit out your first baby at one of these sales and then sell on your baby goods once you've finished with them.

www.nct.org.uk/in-your-area/nearly-new-sales

Specific websites for second-hand...

...maternity clothes

www.mothers2b.co.uk

...gently used premature baby goods

www.earlybaby.co.uk/acatalog/gentlyused.html

...bath stuff, feeding equipment, baby clothes, etc.

www.mymummyandme.co.uk

SURVEYS

Check out www.uksurveypanel.com, which links you to a comprehensive list of online survey sites.

American Consumer Opinion

Win money in monthly draws just for being a member of this market survey group. You can win money in draws when you fill out a 'screener' (a short questionnaire) and get paid each time you complete a 'survey' (a longer questionnaire).

www.acop.com

Opinion Bar

You will earn between £1 and £10 per survey and it's free to join.

www.opinionbar.com

Toluna

With Toluna you get to test goods, give your opinion on them and keep them.

www.toluna.com

Saving Money

There's no time like the present to bag some freebies and switch providers to give yourself the best deal going. Here are some useful cost-cutting resource links.

CHILDCARE

Check out www.hmrc.gov.uk/childcare and talk to your current or any future employers about childcare voucher schemes. By deducting these vouchers before your pay tax you save on your childcare costs.

To work out how other benefits may be affected call the appropriate agency (see page 246).

CARD MAKING

With babies, comes baby friends and that can equal a lot of birthday cards in a year. So to keep your stationery spending down, look into alternative card options rather than rushing straight to the card shop.

DIY cards

Fiona Watt's fantastic book, Making Cards (Art Ideas) features cards for birthdays, Christmas, Easter and Valentine's Day. Every card is clearly and vividly illustrated in an appealing and colourful style, with easy-to-follow, step-by-step instructions.

E-cards

E-cards are a great way to say thank you (or even Happy Birthday, Happy Anniversary or Merry Christmas) for free and can easily be personalised but sent to lots of people quickly. These are my favourites:

www.free-e-cards-online.com
www.ecards.co.uk
www.ecards.msn.co.uk/ecards.aspx
www.bluemountain.com (free for the first month – so perhaps best to join at Christmas)

For a comprehensive list of online e-cards go to:
www.freebielist.com

CHARITY SHOP ONLINE

Oxfam now has its own online shop – so you no longer need to visit the high street for the best bargains.
www.oxfam.org.uk/shop

While you're there, check out its section on hosting Swap It parties for invitations, item tags etc.
www.oxfam.org.uk/get_involved/campaign/activists/swapit.html

FREEBIES

Whether it's via a baby club or a competition, make sure you don't miss out on anything that saves you opening your purse.

Baby Freebies

This site lists free stuff for your baby, for mums-to-be and those who are mums already. It includes links to shops and sites offering discounts, money-off vouchers and news on current deals. Bookmark it and check it each and every month.
www.babyfreebies.co.uk

Boots Parenting Club

Boots Parenting Club is free, easy to join and is open to all UK residents who are pregnant and/or have a child up to the age of two. On joining you will receive a free changing bag and double points on your advantage card when you buy Boots own-brand baby products, Heinz baby food, Pampers Nappies and Wipes, Johnson's toiletries and Philips Avent bottles and sterilisers. You will also receive free parenting magazines, mailings, coupons and vouchers on a regular basis.

www.bootsparentingclub.com

Bounty

On the Bounty website you will find lots of coupons, details of how to receive your goodie packs, freebies, an online community and great competitions. It's quick to join – sign up online or fill in the form in your first Bounty Pack.

www.bounty.com

Hipp Baby Club

Hipp makes organic baby foods and has a great baby club. As a baby club member you'll receive emails throughout your pregnancy and the baby's first year, containing offers, competitions, advice and tips relevant to you and your baby. You'll also be able to create your own personal online baby blog complete with a personalised photo gallery and events calendar.

www.hippbabyclub.co.uk

Huggies Club

If you join the Huggies Club online you are automatically sent £4 worth of vouchers and gain online access to offers and competitions as well as a discussion board. Not bad value for two minutes' work.

www.huggiesclub.com

There are lots more freebie sites. Do a search for 'freebie baby' on www.google.co.uk and see what else you can find.

MORTGAGE ADVICE

This site is produced by the Financial Services Authority – the UK's financial watchdog set up by the government to regulate financial services and protect your rights. The FSA provides clear, impartial information, on this website and in their publications, about financial products and services to help make money matters clearer for you. Unlike almost everyone else they don't try to sell you anything, they just offer simple explanations.

www.moneymadeclear.fsa.gov.uk/mortgages

Alternatively you can call 0845 606 1234, their consumer contact centre, for any general enquiries about financial products and services.

PRICE-COMPARISON WEBSITES

Whether you want to switch electricity providers, find the cheapest car insurance or look for a loan, you can now find everything you need online.

Car insurance

Check out all or some of the following to see if you can save money on your car insurance.

www.gocompare.com
www.comparethemarket.com
www.quotezone.co.uk

Perhaps you'd get a discount at a specialist insurer? Ladybird and Sheila's Wheels just insure women drivers and can often beat your current premium.

0800 977 5012
www.ladybirdinsurance.co.uk

0845 604 3550
www.sheilaswheels.com

Day-to-day expenses

If you're looking to cut the price of your broadband package or your gas bill, then find the best prices online.

www.confused.com
www.ukenergy.co.uk
www.utility-price-comparison.co.uk

Loan or mortgage deals

Maybe your car needs upgrading or you want to switch to a repayment-only mortgage. Whatever the reason, some research done online will reap you dividends for the best deals around. Here are some of those I found useful.

www.moneyexpert.com
www.moneyextra.com
www.moneysavingexpert.com
www.moneysupermarket.com
www.tescocompare.com
www.uswitch.com

For a comprehensive list of loan websites check out www. uk250.co.uk/personalloans.

Petrol prices

Wherever you live, visit this website and it'll tell you the nearest and cheapest petrol prices that day.

www.petrolprices.com.

SPAS

I had a great discount at the spa at one of the Center Parcs (08448 267723 or www.centerparcs.co.uk) but it is well worth calling any spa and asking if they do a pregnancy or new mum rate.

VOUCHER CODES

Some sites have a selection of constantly changing discount voucher codes for anything from clothes and meals out to electrical items and holidays. I suggest you visit them weekly.

www.everydaysale.co.uk
www.myvouchercodes.co.uk
www.vouchercodes.co.uk

Fun and Educational Resources

Many fabulous resources for printables, colouring-in sheets and games exist online and in book form. Here are my favourites, but browse around and find yours.

ACTIVITY VILLAGE

Colouring pages, home schooling and educational resources, kids crafts, puzzles and printables abound at this website; it's particularly good for crafts, parties and themed ideas. And, what's more, it's updated regularly. And it has seasonal resources for specific times or days of the year, such as Earth Day.
www.activityvillage.co.uk

BBC AND CBEEBIES

This fantastic website has craft projects, stories, print and colour sheets and games galore – all are really simple and easy to do and ideal for this age group (up to six years). And if your child has a favourite character, you can hook him in.
www.bbc.co.uk/cbeebies

You can download some great teaching resources from the BBC parenting website.
www.bbc.co.uk/schools/websites/preschool

BOOKTRUST

This website provides free resources and recommendations for teachers, librarians and parents about books for all ages.
www.booktrust.org.uk/books

CRAFT AND ACTIVITY BOOKS

Gill Dickinson, *Crafts for Kids* (London, Hamlyn, 2006).

Marking every kind of special occasion and celebration from Easter to Harvest Festival, Hallowe'en and Christmas, this book shows you how to make colourful and stylish stationery, scented candles, soaps, sweets, masks and lanterns. Each of the 55 projects comes with a list of materials, time taken and age suitability.

Ray Gibson and Amanda Barlow, *The Usborne Big Book of Playtime* (London, Usborne Books, 2003).

This activity book is full of simple things to make and do. It uses step-by-step picture instructions and includes a large range of number skills, such as counting, adding, taking away and sharing. I have played with this (with my children) for hours!

Trish Kuffner, *The Toddler's Busy Book: 365 creative games and activities to keep your one-and-a-half to three-year-old busy* (Minnetonka, Meadowbrook Press, 2008).

This title is packed with activities to keep young children entertained while stimulating their natural curiosity and their physical, mental and emotional growth.

Judy Press and Loretta Trezzo, *Little Hands Art Book: Exploring arts and crafts with 2- to 6-year-olds* (Ideals Publishing Corporation, 2008).

Over 70 art projects with introductory poems to stir kids' imaginations and explore textures, colours, shapes, moods and feelings. Introductions to basic media include glue, doughs, paint, paper, markers and crayons. Parent guidelines are included.

Fretta Reitzes, Beth Teitelman and Lois Alter Mark, *Wonderplay: Interactive and developmental games, crafts, and creative activities for infants, toddlers and preschoolers* (Philadelphia, Running Press, 2007).

Bursting with ideas to enrich the time you spend with your child between birth and the pre-school years, this book divides activities into age-appropriate sections and range from arts and crafts to exercise and drama.

Fiona Watt, *Making Cards (Art Ideas)* (London, Usborne Publishing, 2006).

Usborne Books produces the most fabulous collection of art and craft books; here are just some of my favourites:

50 Things To Draw And Paint
50 Things To Make And Do
Big Book Of Things To Make And Do
Easter Things To Make And Do
How To Draw Animals
How To Draw Dinosaurs
How To Draw Fairies And Mermaids
How To Draw Princesses And Ballerinas
I Can Crayon
I Can Cut And Stick
I Can Draw People
What Shall I Draw?

UNDER 5s

This brilliant and independent UK website promotes pre-school education and provides free resources and information for all early years' providers. Plenty of pre-schools use this amazing website but parents can download learning activities for free, too.

www.under5s.co.uk

My Additional Resource Bank

This section is for you to store any additional useful resources you find. Remember to pass on any treasures.

Name:

Service:

Contact details:

Name:

Service:

Contact details:

Name:

Service:

Contact details:

Name:

Service:

Contact details:

Name:

Service:

Contact details:

Name:

Service:

Contact details:

Name:

Service:

Contact details:

Name:

Service:

Contact details:

Name:

Service:

Contact details:

Name:

Service:

Contact details:

Acknowledgements

I want to thank Jonny for being so strong, working so hard and believing with me in the path we chose to take. You are my best friend and my true love and I am glad you are my babies' daddy and my darling husband. I am so pleased you have been able to spend so much time with us.

I couldn't have done any of this without my wonderful mum, who is always there when I need her, always believes in me and always take great care of me and my children (and often joins in to help me with my crazy schemes). I am proud you are my Mum and my friend, and thank you for all your help. And Dad too, I love you both.

I also want to acknowledge the following extremely special people: Great Grandma, Aunty Jane, Sweeney and Keeley, Helen, Zelga, Linda and John, Sarah B and Sarah C, for all the free lunches, nappies, swimming classes, pre-school sessions, children's clothes, baby clothes, maternity clothes, pots of jam, train rides, football sessions and tennis lessons they have funded and provided. Between you all you have enabled my kids to play well, look fab, eat good food and visit Thomas Land! They have truly been raised by a village. I thank you so much for being so very generous and thoughtful in so many different ways.

For those who read through this book, gave me feedback, were so positive and listened to me rattle on (and on) about my ideas, I am eternally grateful. That's a big hug for Karen, Sarah A, Giselle, AJ and my mum. You are stars.

Many, many, other people have been kind and generous to me and my family in terms of time, energy and gifts – in big and small ways. Thank you, every one of you…you know who you are.

Jennifer Christie, my enthusiastic, positive and inspiring agent, has offered me nothing but support and encouragement, and I cannot thank her enough.

Thanks also to Nikki Sims and Miranda West who edited me so well, and all the staff at Vermilion who have guided this book.

Special thanks also go to: Tracey Winston, Claire Mockbridge and www.kidsexercise.co.uk who gave kind permission for me to quote them in this book.

When the first baby laughed for the first time, the laugh broke into thousands of pieces and they all went skipping about, and that was the beginning of fairies.

from *Peter Pan* by JM Barrie

Index